THE UNSEEN JOURNEY WITHIN YOU

An out-of-the-box approach to unleashing the true YOU

*For all who walk the path of
excitement, curiosity and have
a great attitude towards
LIFE*

THE UNSEEN JOURNEY WITHIN YOU

An out-of-the-box approach to unleashing the true YOU

JASMINKA HANSSON

THE UNSEEN JOURNEY WITHIN YOU
An out-of-the-box approach to unleashing the true YOU

First published in 2018 by
Panoma Press Ltd
48 St Vincent Drive, St Albans, Herts, AL1 5SJ UK

info@panomapress.com
www.panomapress.com

Cover painting by Jasminka Hansson
Cover design by Michael Inns
Artwork by Karen Gladwell

ISBN 978-1-784521-33-2

Printed and bound in Great Britain by TJ International Ltd, Padstow, Cornwall

Testimonials

Jasminka has a beautiful way of telling a story through her unique style and expression. Whether it is through her painting, astrology or writing, she has the ability to expand your mind and shine light on your inner wisdom.

Dr Sarah Hart, *Investor, UK*

It's been 25 years since our paths first crossed, the light of the universe that Jasminka carries lit my path. This book will enlighten others as Jasminka is a true master. Doing the next step with awareness and great understanding.

Sanela Stellnberger, *Professional Home Staging, Austria*

Jasminka is a truth teller. Rarely do you find a person that tells you what you need to hear instead of what you want to hear. With her own unique language/expression, she helps to show how to connect within, gives you insight through astrology of your ultimate potential, and highlights the beauty within you and around you.

Sam Zagami, *Trader, Australia*

Acknowledgements

I AM feeling so much gratitude to my mum for giving me an amazing start in my life, giving me the opportunity to explore and find my journey. To my beautiful seka, my sister, thank you Sabina for being next to me and believing in my crazy adventure. To my incredible husband Mats, my true soulmate who inspires me daily – I love you from here to the universe and back.

To my awesome children Mikaela and Mattias who are the light in my life and show me what really matters; Amelia and Cameron, the most beautiful souls, on their journey of transformation, teaching me that patience and unconditional love can move mountains.

A big thank you to my wonderful friend Lisa, our long discussions about the universe and its energy – I enjoyed every moment and that gave me the inspiration for bringing my words alive. To my special friends Sarah and Sam, thank you both for pushing me to make it happen.

Jo and Steve, my coaches, mentors and friends, you gave me the opportunity to step up and believe in myself – thank you from the bottom of my heart.

Thank you Mindy, my publisher, and your amazing team for your superb structure and guidance, giving me the confidence to make my dream a reality... supporting, helping and inspiring others... everything and anything is possible!

Finally, a massive thank you to all the beautiful souls who have been part of my journey from the beginning of my life till now that I had the privilege to meet, learn from and expand my horizon ... your lives have been my inspiration and my reward.

Thank you... love you all

Contents

The meaning of the dragonfly: in almost every part of the world the dragonfly symbolises change, a change that has its source in mental and emotional maturity; a deeper understanding of the meaning of life. The association with water and with a dragonfly flying across water, represents going beyond what is on the surface... looking into the deeper implications and aspects of life.

Introduction

I WAS born in Croatia, raised in Vienna and moved to Dorset in England. As early as I can remember, I asked myself: Who am I, why am I here, why are these my parents, why do I live in Vienna? I was also quite fascinated about planets, stars, our universe, the cosmos.

My father passed away when I was 21 years old. Through my emotional pain and looking for answers I came across astrology and I loved it. In my mind it all made sense, the universal energy that gives us life and leads us to our true potential. I started to understand my journey from birth and further, my challenges, my weaknesses and strengths, the universal cycles and the opportunity for growth with awareness.

At this time, in my mid-twenties, my creativity and expression in colours became more real. I also started working on myself with psychosynthesis, family constellation, shamanism and later with holotropic breathwork (www.holotropic-association.eu). It felt like taking off layers that were built for protection.

Psychological Astrology became part of my life. It is a helpful tool, a great insight into ourselves, a much richer approach to life.

To become who you really are, to take some heavy layers off and to be your authentic self, there is a journey and action that has to be taken, step by step, up the hill and down the hill, big mountains and strong rivers, through darkness and light, through cold and heat, alone and in company... every colour of life but also black and white, I call it a colourful roller coaster. This book will give you guidance, structure and confirmation:

- ❧ **for certain feelings that you kept for yourself and wanted to express but didn't know how to**
- ❧ **answers for your unspoken questions**
- ❧ **a better understanding for your being here and now**
- ❧ **great tools for moving forward**

Life is full of challenges and that is what makes it such a profound learning experience.

The more you are consciously in touch with yourself, the more life will offer – beautiful surprises, great gifts and an inner growth that is almost unimaginable.

I am inviting you to meet yourself... an opportunity for your unique personal transformation.

> *'The individual may strive after perfection but must suffer from the opposite of his intentions for the sake of his completeness.'*
>
> - C.G. Jung -

It is time to look inside and take action...

I don't know. Do you know? Is it time to look inside and take action? Perhaps, maybe, possibly... I really don't know! What I do know is that:

- ✑ **without action there is no movement**
- ✑ **without action there is no achievement and definitely no rewards and no legacy leaving behind**

Yes, it comes with some effort and yes, it is not easy to make change happen. However, action is necessary and vital for manifesting the dream into reality.

I have been there, you have been there, everyone has been there, where no action was wanted – because it is easier to stay in the same old whatever!

If you do the same, you get the same.

Today is the day to take action and look inside...

Yes I **can** do it
Yes I **will** do it
Yes I **am** doing it
and

Today I am **going** to reach out and take action
Today I **will** reach out and take action
Today I *am* reaching out to do so

*'A journey of a thousand miles begins
with one single step.'*

- Laotse -

CHOOSE LIFE

CHAPTER ONE

Life Forms Your Own
Tools For Moving Forward

LIFE BRINGS challenges and these challenges are vital for our own growth. Without challenges we would not be able to grow and move forward. Challenges come in all kind of shapes and forms, appear in events and people. Challenges come into our lives to shake us up, wake us up from our long or just a short sleep – asking and pushing for a change of the situation that we are in at this moment. It is time to get up on our feet and start to make a move! Even a little move, a tiny step, will bring a change in this challenging situation.

We felt already that something is bothering us, making us feel restless, or the opposite, making us feel tired, no energy and no motivation whatsoever; feelings of loss, frustration, anger, fear, insecurity are appearing on a regular basis... it might be in our relationship, or work, family, finances, health etc. An issue in an area in our life that needs to be looked at a bit closer. Simply it does need attention and yes it feels uncomfortable. It would be much easier to put the head in the sand and pretend it will go away. Actually, it will not – sorry! It will still be here until we face it and start to recognise it.

We are all different and of course we will approach it all in different ways and there are 101 ways to see a challenge and experience a challenge. Only one step forwards with our unique approach will start to change something and the discomfort of our emotions, which are getting more and more out of control, will change into something different. Being in a different space will bring different results.

With time these different results will turn into opportunities. This is somehow where the magic starts... we are forced to look inside and ask these certain questions. The first one usually starts with 'Why me?' yes, 'why me?' This is a victim question, a feeling of being the victim and blaming everyone around us; our inner whole becomes emptier. Actually, if we listen very carefully, there is a voice deep inside and a voice of courage is screaming in silence 'enough is enough'; slowly but surely the challenge is trying to turn into an opportunity.

Remember, we all see an opportunity in different ways and approach it in different ways: some grab it and run with it, some take it slow to feel the safety of doing the right thing. At least some different results are coming to light. However, this new experience is forming a tool, a tool to deal with the challenge in front of us with courage, bravery and love. With time this tool will take shape that is visible to you but also it is created only by you. It sits in you, deep in you to be discovered and it will help you on the path of your journey, to learn more about yourself... how to deal with certain issues on the way, and really to become aware of the challenges and turn them into opportunities. This tool, made by you, is unique and will follow you your whole lifetime.

I would like to share one of my challenges that might give you a better understanding.

My challenge took me to the darkest places and of course the suffering and my emotions were heavy on my shoulders. When I shared my situation with friends and family, I only heard that it was our fault, meaning me and my husband. OK, it wasn't encouraging at all and of course it did not help us. It just started all the negative feelings to be highlighted. My husband and I have a business together and we went through a huge change, almost like a transformation in itself. It was a bit like a massive hurricane coming through our life and destroyed the foundation of our business. It was time to do something different and we asked for help and received just that – a great support from the outside, meaning we met an amazing couple and they became our mentors and coaches. However, the finances were not improving how we wished or actually how I would have liked.

There were many times of 'enough is enough' and still I was unable to see the core of my challenge. Step by step, my questions led towards something very interesting. I discovered the word 'value'. I started to look at my own self-worth, my own value towards myself and asked, how much do I value myself? What does value mean to me? Why does self-worth feel uncomfortable?

The real meaning of value comes from the inside and not from the outside. I realised that I had quite a bit of difficulty with this topic. On one hand if I don't value myself how can people value me, on the other hand if people value me and I don't value myself it is not solving it either. It took me a while to understand that it is my doing that I need to look a bit closer into myself. It was time to do something different. The first step was to respect myself and to build a pride for my actions *and* honour my achievements. Value is linked with money. If I don't value myself how can I receive money, how can I take money? My challenge became the opportunity to look closer into myself and see more clearly into my true values. How do I value myself?

Stepping up and valuing ourselves for who we are. Through time, the tool, in this case 'value' will take shape and it is only formed by us. We are our own blacksmith. It does depend how we form and shape our own tools. Our personality plays a big role.

a) The Understanding Of Our Personality Which Plays A Significant Role For Shaping The Life Tools

I would like to take you to another level of understanding, the bigger picture of our play and existence through universal law/cosmic rules. Let me explain and take you through a journey with an interesting view of our being. That will bring some insight as to why we do certain things a certain way, shaping and forming our life tools. Are you ready?

Each one of us has a unique approach towards life, it depends on our blueprint, our 'make-up', our DNA. Some are quick in making decisions, some take forever to move forward, some are big dreamers, some just go with the flow, some need support from others, some like to do it alone, etc. A bit like the elements fire, earth, air and water and the cycles of our own life on Mother Earth and the universe. What I mean is... let's explain it in simple words:

- ❧ some naturally have more fire energy and are able to push quicker to achieve their purpose
- ❧ with the earth energy these are more grounded and approach life step by step
- ❧ some with air energy are big thinkers and can think through 101 times to fulfil a task
- ❧ with the water energy these people like to dream and go with the flow

Each one has a unique mixture, more or less, of these elements in their own blueprint. This is why we are all special and unique, no one is the same, and the shape and form of our tools too.

OK, let's move on further, and stay with me...

b) The Understanding And Effect Of The Universal Cycles

Our life approaches us with certain cycles, that brings challenges and pushes us to turn it into opportunities.

First – *Our awareness, our personality, our strengths and weaknesses will lead us to our inner sources.*

Second – *Naturally, we long to have a solid foundation in our lives either for us or one day for our family, also to have security and a feeling of safety. Yes, we make sure that our fundamental rules and structures are in place to be able to achieve our basic needs.*

Third – *We are our own teacher and leader but also our own architect and builder.*

OK, so these roles will be activated through cycles, and we will experience these cycles, the cosmic rules, at certain times in our life. Each one of these cycles has their own purpose to be achieved and fulfilled. Some take a few weeks and some can take many years. OK, as above, so in us. I will explain it in more detail to bring some common sense into that kind of understanding.

The beginning of a cycle starts with something new, like an idea. This something new comes and stays with you. With time this idea that you created or it just popped up or maybe even you picked it up by reading something etc. will be challenged and tested if it is still OK for you, if it still resonates with you. With time you will have doubts and questions. When everything is filtered through, tested and approved by you, this idea becomes reality and is ready to be taken to the next level.

Let's explain it a bit more in a simple way, how it happens in reality. So, you have a vision and somehow this vision becomes one with you. This vision is big and doesn't let go of you. This vision is the beginning of a cycle, a bit like a seed that you plant for yourself. You are all excited and really going for it. You share it with the whole world, meaning your family, your friends, your colleagues, everyone needs to know about your vision, your unique discovery. The 'I' wants to shout!

Then time goes by... you feel doubt and no one is listening to your vision anymore. The excitement starts to fade! With this isolation, a feeling of loneliness and separation will lead to discomfort. Time passes and pushes and pulls you with questions where you ask yourself, hmmm, is this a dream, just a dream, perhaps I am just dreaming and fooling myself?

After the doubts and the feeling of discomfort and rejection, the mature/grown-up conversation kicks in. A dialogue between your subconscious and conscious figuring out what the big dream is really about. You start to filter through the good and not so good bits and the essence of the vision is still in you. The time is approaching for you to let go of everything that doesn't fit your vision 100%. The real essence of your vision is filtering through, gets more clarity and structure. A new excitement, a new 'step-up' is ready to be taken and planted on another level.

Everyone is going through these cycles of life. You can use it for any topic – let's use relationship. You imagine a fantastic awesome person. This person enters your life and you are all love, heart and passion – an amazing 'honeymoon' period, you can't get enough of each other. After a while, when the reality kicks in, this person starts to challenge you, even shutting down some parts of your personality. You might think, awww, I still do feel love, but the honeymoon period is disappearing slowly. With time the real 'I' is knocking on the door, eventually asking 'who am I? Is this what I want or is this how I imagined it?' The opposite is approaching you, pushing and pulling the truth out of you. Either you take the step and change the situation with awareness or you let it go for good!

When you managed to get the essence of the relationship and sailed through these opposites between two people, you start to feel more alive and see the true potential between you two. It is time to filter through what this relationship is all about and let go of the old beliefs and get ready for the next chapter. A new seed is ready to be planted, a more mature relationship with more experience in this field.

Another example on a bigger scale of how these cycles express themselves. There are quite a few of them, some over a short period of time and some over a long period of time. Each one of us is experiencing these movements in our lives. One of them is the seven-year cycle that will make sure that our inner foundation and our inner structure is built carefully and strongly, preparing itself for being destroyed by another cycle that comes along. On one hand we build this strong foundation, which brings safety and security, but on the other hand the 'attraction' lies in becoming too set in our ways, feeling too comfortable.

If you believe it or not, our inner growth does naturally need space for expansion and movement. Subconsciously we are ready for the next cycle that will bring sudden changes and revolutionise breakthroughs for each of us in different forms i.e. events, people, loss, work promotion, marriage, family – **life** in its own glory and in all shades of colours. This next cycle is putting us in touch with unexplored parts of our nature. It shows that we are ready to break out of our routines and our own patterns, laid by our past, which are becoming too rigid and old.

It is time to shed the skin, it is time to build a bigger 'house' for the soul to expand and experience new challenges, it is time to grow taller and see what is in front, it is time to let go of the old and enter the new.

c) The Benefits Of These Life Cycles

At these cycles which bring crises, difficulties, problems, challenges, opportunities, possibilities, big changes, sudden changes, a feeling of being 'forced', it is a good time to connect with yourself. When you seek your attention towards yourself it will create a loving relationship in and with you. It will lead to awareness of kindness and compassion at these important and challenging times in your life. This special relationship with yourself will bring you closer to you. Having this close relationship one to one, you and you only, getting to know and perhaps to understand more about you:

- what you like and dislike
- what you need and do not need
- what you want and do not want
- what is important and not important
- what you are looking for and not looking for anymore

is definitely helping you further to your inner fulfilment, creating a feeling of respect, self-value and self-worth.

d) Help And Support Through Some Simple Exercises

Let's take you to some simple exercises to help you to go through these universal cycles positively and focused.

We are surrounded by beautiful gifts from Mother Earth, which are free and ready to be acknowledged, that could be implemented in our daily life. At these challenging times we can turn to Mother Earth and connect with these gifts ...

THE ELEMENTS

The meaning of the elements and their power/energy simply explained:

FIRE – *the sun is the life force and gives us vitality.*
Through music and dance we are able to express the inner fire, the passion, the drama and activate our inner drive to action our dream, the vision.

EARTH – *a physical energy that forces us to be and stay grounded.*
Through regular exercise e.g. cycling, running, swimming, walking etc. simple and basic movements will give our dreams stability and put them into reality.

AIR – *a positive mind with a great attitude can move mountains.*
Being outside daily and breathing fresh air, smelling the beauty that surrounds us, will clear the mind from worries, waste and negativity and lead the focus towards the bigger picture.

WATER – *the flow of life.*
Any water... sea, river, lake etc. will bring calmness and stillness to the soul.

MEDITATION

Through regular meditation our whole being connects to our inner source where we can recharge our batteries for gaining inner harmony and relaxation.

The meditation will give you the opportunity to connect with the elements consciously by spending a moment with the energy and yourself.

Before you prepare yourself, just a little note. I know that we are all busy and lead a busy life. I know that time is very precious to all of us and it has to be handled with care. I will just say if we spend time with the right attitude, the achievement will be enormous and it will be rewarded with great opportunities. There is no need to do all of them at once. Choose one that you feel attracted to, one that you feel more curious about or just go with the flow. Each element will bring something special and unique. We will resonate with one more than the other. So, no worries which one comes first or second! Whatever you choose, it will be the right one for you at this moment... perhaps it is time to trust your gut feeling.

I would like to mention as well when doing this exercise please don't expect too much straight away and don't worry if you don't see any pictures or some magical feelings appearing in yourself. Be authentic and let the flow take you. It will take some time to start to feel relaxed completely. So, please be kind to yourself and have patience. At the beginning, at this stage, it is more important to get used to this kind of feeling of breathing and letting go, clearing the mind as much as possible and exploring your inner flow and **you**, the way you 'tick'! With time and taking this exercise as a routine, daily, weekly or monthly, you will have a different outlook and a better understanding of yourself.

So, let's go back to basics, you will need a notebook. I mean it would be great to start to have your own journal where you write your ideas, dreams, experiences – actually everything and anything that comes your way. Also, if you like to express in painting or drawing, you should have a pen, pencils, all kind of colours in watercolours, crayons etc. and paper either coloured or white. Whatever you have at home you can use and experiment with it. If you think painting and writing is not your style you could use old magazines, catalogues, newspapers etc. You could cut out pictures, words, letters etc. and anything else you could think of to start to express your creativity. The flow of your creativity is limitless. Remember to let go from restrictions and boundaries, expectations and perfection. Let's play and have some fun!

F I R E

Find a place in your home where you feel comfortable and relaxed. It would be good to have some fresh air in the room before you start your special 'me time'. Make sure that no one will interrupt your special time and the mobile phone is switched off, really turned off and away from you, far away! Wear some comfortable clothes so you can move freely. Choose a soft relaxing music – music without words, only sound. Words will interrupt your flow and your mind will start to listen to the words only.

So, put your music on, for example meditation, classical music, something that will bring your mood into a 'floppy' state… you choose, there are no rules. Your aim is to feel comfortable and relaxed. Find your own position. I recommend to lie on the floor, on a mat or blanket, because you are staying grounded the whole time, your body is naturally in a relaxing position and you don't need to hold yourself up as you would do when sitting. Lie on your back straight and legs straight with your arms close to your body and hands open, facing towards the ceiling. Please don't use a pillow, keep your body really straight and firm on the floor. The energy will flow much easier. You can try it yourself and see the difference. Make sure you have a blanket next to you just in case you start feeling a bit cold (this is usually me!).

When you are ready, breathe in and breathe out, aim to have your mind and your body relaxed, so breathe in and out a few times and let go, let go of everything around you, let go of your inner tension on your shoulders, arms, legs, your whole body, your thoughts, your worries and your timetable of getting stuff done – again breathe in and breathe out.

When you feel all relaxed, imagine the sun, the provider of all life, breathe into the golden light from the sun, the warmth that is coming through you, breathe in and breathe out. Stay in this golden light of warmth for a moment, this golden light is transforming into golden fire and spreading out in your whole body, put your mind in the space of the element of fire – bonfire, volcano, the sun etc.

Observe what is happening in your mind, any pictures, what is coming towards you and go with it, enjoy the ride of strength, confidence and pure energy that gives you the power to do your actions, your steps to achieve your own dreams, your amazing unique dream. Even if you have to scream, shout, go crazy, or even cry – let go of all your limitations and be fire; move if you have to move, dance if you have to dance, scream if you have to scream, or even just be, whatever comes naturally, go with the flow. The inner fire, your own fire that you have access to, wants to be visible.

Stay as long as you can in this feeling and when you are ready, come back into here and now. Stay in this moment of here and now, take it in and don't get up straight away. Make sure you are fully back and grounded by breathing in and out a few times. If you feel an urge to express it on paper, do so. You have prepared everything and it is all in front of you. Let your creativity lead you and enjoy, enjoy what you have experienced, stay in this moment as long as you can – it is all you, your unique you.

E A R T H

The same as before, your own space, no interruption, no mobile phone, some fresh air in the room before you start. Choose your own space, make yourself comfortable, have a blanket on the side, just in case. Put your music on and let go, breathe in and breathe out a few times.

Every time you breathe out you imagine that your mind is free of all worries and concerns, it is just you and yourself. Breathe in the earth, imagine the earth, the ground, the soil, our trees, the smell of the flowers, nature, the sound of birds, bees... whatever comes naturally to you, go with the flow, feel yourself grounded, feel yourself being one with Mother Earth that provides you with the nourishment, being the tree, being the flower, your roots are connecting with the earth. These roots are grounding you and staying strong and healthy, protecting and supporting you. Stay with it and feel your strength and your roots, really take it in, fully in.

Stay as long as you can in this grounded feeling and when you are ready, come back into here and now. Take this experience and write it down, stay in the flow, let your creativity lead you, enjoy yourself and your strong roots – it is all you, your special you.

A I R

The same as before, your own space with no clutter from the outside, no interference, just you and yourself. Don't forget to switch off the mobile phone and have a blanket next to you, just in case you feel cold or have the desire to spend more time in your environment of your amazing energy. Put your relaxation music on and make yourself comfortable by lying down. Breathe in and breathe out a few times. Each time you breathe in fill your tummy with air. Breathe out and make your tummy empty, do this a few times the same, fill your tummy with air, tummy out of air. Imagine the air is filling your whole body, in and out. Fresh air is coming through you. Pure clean air is filling your lungs, your body and your mind. It takes all your worries away from you. The fresh air with its beautiful smell that surrounds you is taking you to your journey of dreams, big visions and beauty in all colours.

Stay in this vibrant place and explore your creation of your dream, the endless opportunity of possibilities. Look around and take it in. Breathe in this feeling as much as you can. Enjoy this beauty that you created in your mind and stay as long as you want. When you are ready, come back into here and now. Take this experience and express it the way that comes naturally to you – it is all you, your awesome you.

W A T E R

The last element in this exercise. You are in your special place, your music is ready, no one is interrupting you and the mobile phone is far away from you and switched off. You feel comfortable in your lying position with the blanket next to you. Your chosen meditation music is on. Breathe in and breathe out, and again breathe in and breathe out a few more times. Imagine water is flowing next to you. The sound of water is surrounding you. Breathe in very deeply and let go, let go of everything that is around you. It is only you and the water. The sound of water is making you feel calm and completely relaxed, a feeling of cleansing, washing away the heaviness and discomfort that is pulling you away from yourself. A feeling of pureness and lightness is taking over your body, entering your inner source, your own inner well. Imagine your own golden cup, your Holy Grail, is sitting next to the well, waiting for you, have a sip of this pure clean water, enjoy the sip slowly, really slowly, cleansing you from the inside, washing away all the tension.

Stay at your well and feel the surroundings, the calmness and stillness that is taking over you. Enjoy the peace and the harmony. When you are ready, come back into here and now. Breathe in and out and stay focused. Take this experience and express it the way you feel like – it is all you, your beautiful you.

When you are finished with these exercises have a look at your creations, your work that **you** produced. Respect and honour it fully. You did amazingly well to open up to your inner self and let go. You dived very deep to find the connection and being able to bring it to reality, bring it alive.

As you can see, there are no rules and no expectations. Just follow your gut feeling, your instinct, your intuition and let go from everything around you if you can. With time, if you do it regularly, it will become much easier and you can tune into it much quicker. There will be perhaps one element where you might feel a real connection; it might feel more profound to you. It just shows you that this element has a bigger play in your life and it can be of great help for your achievements when you enter situations with some difficulties. You can connect with these elements at any time if you need help or support on your journey. When action is required you connect with the sun; if a situation needs grounding you imagine the earth element; when your mind is full of stuff you imagine air; and if you feel drained and exhausted water exercise will bring calmness and peace.

Practising these elements or even imagining it, the feeling that you experienced while doing the exercise will become a part in and of you. Your notebook with your detailed expressions and your creations that were born at this moment, spread them out around you or keep them close to you. It is up to you, what really feels comfortable.

RITUALS

Rituals are an important part of life; it is a celebration and is allowing quality time – a timetable designed only for 'me time'. This is the time where you are allowing yourself to connect with your inner source, where you recharge your batteries. It would be great to practise and make it a habit. Even a short moment of here and now brings a feeling of relaxation and peace... me time! A repetition becomes a habit and leads to inner strength, and that leads to confidence. With this amazing inner fulfilment you inspire yourself and that will lead you to inspire others. You become a role model by being authentic and true to yourself, for others at home, at work, in your community and in the world.

I would like to give you a few examples, so you have an idea how you can use these exercises outside your home when needed to get back to your true self and how beneficial these exercises can become if you connect with your conscious. You are the source for all your steps needed. With kindness and the knowledge of what is important for you and to you, you just connect with these elements. Working with Mother Nature will bring abundance and remind you that you are part of it. Amazing, isn't it?!

e) The Practical Way

So, let's share some ideas on how it works in reality, the practical way.

I was on a seminar and it was a lot to take in. Not much movement and mainly sitting, concentrating and focusing on the tasks. I felt very tired and drained. At lunchtime I felt the need to be grounded somehow. I needed to come back to earth because my mind was full of words, my brain was 'smoking'. There was a little park next to where the seminar was being held and I thought that is perfect. Knowing my need of grounding I decided to lean against a tree. I closed my eyes and imagined myself connecting with the roots of the tree, breathing in and breathing out a few times and I stayed for a moment in blissful stillness. It took me only a few minutes and I felt energised already. I gave thanks, I felt grateful for the gift that was given to me.

Another example – when feeling rigid and boxed up...

... meaning everything is too structured or too closed up, it is time to open up and look beyond these limitations. I am lucky to live very close to the sea. I take a few moments to connect with this beautiful surrounding, breathing in and breathing out a few times and I am imagining that this view is approaching my spirit and is taking off my boundaries and opening my view to my limitless creativity. Everything is possible. I am the creator not the limiter. So are you, you are the creator not the limiter. Feeling grateful for this beautiful gift from Mother Nature.

With fire energy – a great idea is...

There are times when I feel completely low and not able to get up, especially in the morning. One morning I just thought to pull my duvet over my head and stay in that position forever! Of course, we all know it doesn't work, I am sure a lot of us experienced that kind of morning laziness... 101 things are waiting for us to be activated, cared for, looked at, etc. I have a little Sonos sound system and one of my favourite radio channels is Superfly FM (Vienna radio channel, it is nightclub music for grown-ups). I just push the button and here comes my music with great vibration and makes me jump straight away into a dancing mood. Some great dancing moves ... I am the dancing queen, and the world is ready for my actions. Excitement and happiness is all over my body, soul, spirit...

Mind energy is a different story...

How it works for me is my mind needs structure and being organised. When it comes to chaos and confusion in my mind I do two things: writing my thoughts down in my notebook (as you have hopefully started already) and making some space for new ideas and letting go from nagging thoughts. Sometimes I need to unclutter my home and put some organisation in place. However, the main thing, and the quickest, is to step out into the garden, if you have one, if not just open the window. I look up to the sky and breathe in and breathe out a few times and connect with it. I let go and let go and let go of my thoughts. I breathe in clarity, the air, the oxygen that is part of Mother Earth, that breaks through my confusion and chaos. Thanking it for giving me clarity and actually it is also a reminder that breathing from the tummy has not to be forgotten!

As you can see, you can connect anywhere –
at your home, outside, while travelling, abroad
or even when shopping.

It takes only a few minutes and it brings you right back to yourself. Practise and experiment where and how you can use your inner source to connect and recharge your battery, so you can and will approach life with authenticity and full of great positive energy.

Be creative... these are your tools made
by you to perfection

What you give yourself will shine through to the outside.

View at *www.jasminkahansson.com*

I AM LIFE

CHAPTER TWO

Trust And Believe
In Yourself

THIS IS easier said than done... and it sounds too simple! I know, but actually it is that simple. Our mind is very powerful, really powerful and we have to be careful what we put in our mind. Be aware what vocabulary you are using, what kind of words are travelling from you to others. Each word has energy and this energy is around you all the time. It does depend on what language we use. Each word has its own frequency. Positive words travel in higher frequencies and negative words in lower frequencies. So, how do we express ourselves? What language do we use to be heard and understood? Interesting, isn't it?! Imagine what would happen using higher frequency words – how would our surroundings be? Then imagine, what would happen using lower frequency words... ?

a) The Water Experiment

I don't know if you know the experiment with the water and the plant. There has been research done on water whereby if you talk positively, nice strong beautiful words and spreading love, the water will receive these high frequencies and will transform into beautiful stars, and it stays clean and pure. If you talk in negative sentences the water turns into a stain, dark coloured and stays muddy. Interesting, isn't it?

Our body is made of approximately 70% water. Let's go a bit further – all organs contain quite a bit of water:

❧ **the brain and heart are 73% water**

❧ **the lungs are about 83% water**

❧ **the skin contains 64% water**

❧ **the muscles and kidneys are 79% water**

❧ **and even the bones are a watery 31%**

(Data: The Water Science School)

So, what does it tell you?

It tells you that the frequency will go whatever you do. Your body will become either clean and pure or stained and dark. It will influence your wellbeing and the people around you. Your positive inside, being in this high frequency state, will of course shine through to the outside. Great, isn't it? How powerful this little insight is. It can change your wellbeing in an instant. Love it!

The other experiment where I think it is amazing too is talking to plants. Yes, talking to plants. In this case a houseplant. My friend Lisa actually tried it and I was amazed to hear the outcome. She put two little plants in the kitchen: one was looked after and cared for with love, the other was ignored and left alone. She did the watering as usual but the talking and connecting daily in two ways:

CB **giving attention to one plant**

CB **ignoring the other one**

Guess what? In a short period of time she could see the difference. Yes, the plant with love was growing and flowering beautifully and the other plant without love and being ignored unfortunately became lifeless. You can try it yourself if you wish, the outcome will put a smile on your face.

b) Our Powerful Mind

Our mind is very powerful!
Our mind can be smart and effective
Our mind can move mountains...
... and it can find you a great parking space
when needed!

Just a quick example to share with you:

When being short of time, busy and running around like a headless chicken and doing shopping at the same time... hmm, it can be quite tricky to find a parking space. When I go to my local Waitrose, the parking spaces are really tiny and mainly full. Before I enter the car park, actually while I am driving, I am focused to find the perfect parking space and see myself finding a space. There are three great car spots and guess what, I almost always get one of these spaces – if not the first then the second best. What I am saying is that the mind is sooooo powerful and can do anything, even give you a perfect car parking spot. Try it out yourself ... focus and imagine it, see it and it is done!

Yes, our mind can move mountains but also, unfortunately, it can destroy our achievements too, in a heartbeat. To move mountains it takes time, persistence, patience, commitment and action; to destroy something it can be done in seconds.

You always have the choice – everything
is in your hands!

The choice is yours and choose wisely!

One of the most powerful words that has a strong and beautiful frequency is gratitude.

Being grateful and giving love without expecting anything back.

Being grateful for what we have here and now and what we have achieved already in us and around us... it is quite powerful.

A little ritual that I use daily that I would like to share with you, a little gift of awareness from me to you:

ॐ Every morning when I get up I say with a deep consciousness, with respect and a feeling of gratitude, 'Good morning' (if the sun is out I look at the sun and almost bow down in silence, inside myself, feeling grateful for giving me life and purpose).

ॐ Every evening when I go to bed, the last thing in my mind, I say with a deep consciousness, with respect and a feeling of gratitude 'Good night' (if the moon is visible I look at the moon and thank her for the opportunities given to me and to my loved ones).

It would be so wonderful to have that kind of awareness and be able to observe our actions daily, our behaviour towards others and ourselves. How easily excuses are found by saying 'I can't do it', 'Not now', 'I will do it tomorrow' but we are also easily distracted to do something completely different that is not relevant to us at all, just wasting and killing time, like searching the web and looking on Facebook, reading the gossip in certain magazines, watching silly mindless TV programmes etc. We all know that! I am sure we all have a long list of excuses and distractions.

Having and receiving compassion from the outside is nice – really just nice and it stays just nice! We like to bathe in the energy of feeling sorry for ourselves, playing the victim and leaving it for tomorrow or even another day. However, by being honest, really honest with yourself and in yourself will bring clarity. Eventually that will lead to action. Step by step moving in a direction which feels right at this exact moment. But also allowing yourself, giving yourself the permission, that it is OK to make mistakes and experience failure. Without mistakes and failure there is no learning...

Very simple: 'no mistakes no learning.'

These experiences present us with the knowledge and confidence how to do it and how not to do it the next time.

If you do the same you will get the same.

Only by doing, moving and being in action will we start to embrace our trust and belief system that is lying in us already. It is an important part of our growth by being in movement emotionally and mentally on a regular basis. With time a feeling of pride and achievement will appear from the inside. A celebration of these little or big achievements would be great to put in place. It is a celebration, your recognition of being amazing, being appreciated by you, that **you** did the first steps and **you** put it in action, no one else only **you**. A little 'well done me' will do perfectly. However, there will be days where we don't want to see the sun around us and/or inside us, and we choose instead to feel or have:

֍ **the urge to mislead ourselves**

֍ **to be the victim**

֍ **to have and look for compassion from the outside**

- ⊗ to feel very sorry for ourselves
- ⊗ to keep our head in the sand
- ⊗ to repeat the same dilemma, the same story

The fear of failing, the fear of not being perfect or good enough, holds us back from going forward, and yes, not allowing ourselves to do these important steps to fail and make mistakes on our journey. Only these steps of these experiences, having a certain amount of failures, will lead us forward. An inside wisdom is created, that knowing 'if I am untrue to myself I will feel tension, discomfort and pain'. We need to 'hurt' ourselves or to feel hurt so we can step-up. We need to walk on all fours sometimes, so we know how to get up and stand up. Without these experiences there is no shaping of our tool that I mentioned before. This is where trust comes in, to trust ourselves whatever we do, to trust that we know exactly where we have to go.

Believing in you is the most beautiful gift that you can give yourself.

Through that fundamental foundation of 'trust and believe' we will do what has to be done. If we can let go of all limits, in and outside, life would be much easier. These limits are trying to pin us down. When we let go and embrace the inner feeling of trust and belief, our gut feeling, we are able to do the necessary steps for moving towards our dream, our vision... to our self or what is important for us at that moment.

So, please consider and be aware of your behaviour:

- ❦ the words that form the language of optimism are kindness and gratitude 'the glass is half full'

- ❦ or is it the opposite by being the pessimist 'the glass is half empty', the 'I want' or simply blaming others and not taking the responsibility for the action?

- ❦ does it happen on a regular basis or just here and there?

- ❦ what kinds of words are forming the thoughts and the mind?

- ❦ how do we talk to others and ourselves?

Please step back for a moment and reflect:

- ❦ which language comes naturally to you?
- ❦ which words of energy are naturally expressed?
- ❦ is it 'the glass half *full* or 'the glass half *empty*?

I leave this one with you!

The awareness becomes important, actually very important. **It is vital!** Each word has energy that is positive and negative. The effect that will carry us through on our path. The power lies in these words. Positive frequencies will lead to feeling and becoming confident.

> *With time and taking action regularly towards*
> *a goal that you have created,*
>
> *a dream, a vision that you have in yourself deep inside,*

your true purpose of being authentic

that is somewhere hidden perhaps most of the time.

However, with awareness and being truly conscious
of your actions...

... will make it happen

I would like to share a story with you that will give you an idea of what I am trying to explain. My babies were born at home, actually in the bathroom. Everyone was against my wish (of course, as they are when we are doing something 'crazy' in other people's eyes, in their opinion). When having a clear vision, a dream and being able to step out of the crowd, a crowd that we think will provide support and safety... think twice! My husband and I started to implement certain steps towards the vision of a home birth and providing the safety and beauty to welcome the spirit into the world. Only my inner trust and strong belief in myself led me to achieve what I put out. I had doubts, of course, and big fears and on top 101 'ifs'. I stayed true to myself and did everything in my power to make it happen. There was no space for negativity or for someone from the outside to take my wish away.

I put all the actions in place and focused on researching, reading, attending weekend workshops (water birth, Janet Balaskas), pregnancy yoga, meditation, healthy eating, being active etc. – everything that was necessary to feel confident and powerful in myself. Also to mention, naturally I am not good with pain at all. I can't take pain! Still, I only focused on the outcome that everything would be perfect, exactly the way that I imagined it. My plan B was in place: if, yes the word 'if', only one 'if' – if something would, could, might happen, it would be taken care of. In my mind nothing was going to happen of course. I trusted and believed 100% and I knew deep inside, a very strong confirmation, everything was going to be just fine. My deep wish was to create a perfect entrance for the spirit that had chosen me to come to Mother Earth... a quote from Kahlil Gibran inspired me many years ago, stayed with me and will stay with me forever.

With trust and belief, with certain actions, staying focused, a positive healthy mind, natural movement, preparation, persistence, commitment, patience and time – only you can make it happen!

Also to mention when making a commitment for achieving the vision, there are sacrifices to make especially when deciding for parenthood. In this case, giving birth. It is not about you and your needs anymore, it is all about the spirit and the welcome to Mother Earth. A lot of research had to be done for me to feel comfortable, what I needed to do, not what others were telling me to do. There is a lot of stuff out there, so be aware and look closely. It has to resonate with you. The physical and emotional side has to be looked at much closer and dealt with in a mature, grown-up and straightforward manner. You have to be fit physically and mentally and to do your certain exercises, gentle exercises daily. Not to forget the food intake – what you eat and how you eat. It is a very important part to be considered too, so be very honest, realistic and very clear with yourself. It is not about you, it is about the spirit. It is a preparation for you, your body and your mind – a detox on all levels – making the womb ready on all levels for the arrival. It takes time, full commitment, routines and focus.

This is the quote:

Your children are not your children.
They are the sons and daughters of life's
longing for itself.

They come through you but not from you, and though
they are with you, yet they belong not to you.

You may give them your love but not your thoughts.
For they have their own thoughts.

You may house their bodies but not their souls,
for their souls dwell in the house of tomorrow,
which you cannot visit, not even in your dreams.

You may strive to be like them, but seek
not to make them like you.

For life goes not backward nor tarries with yesterday.

You are the bows from which your children as living arrows
are sent forth. The archer sees the mark upon the path of the

infinite, and He bends you with His might that His arrows may go swift and far. Let your bending in the archer's hand be for gladness; For even as He loves the arrow that flies, so He loves also the bow that is stable.

- Kahlil Gibran -

Times like these are very profound when we work so closely together in harmony with this gut feeling of reassurance and a massive inner drive of achieving the big vision. At these times we have ourselves as the best friend. Our own best friend will give support, help, courage, encouragement, love, compassion, honesty, gratitude, kindness, exactly the way we need it. Everything is on our side, no one, really no one is able to take our set mission away. There is so much trust and belief in and from our self that will move mountains in any sizes and shapes.

We all know the expression 'You are your best friend or you are your worst enemy.'

It is very true and fits so perfectly in this picture!

c) The Awareness Of Family Patterns

Then we approach times where everyone is against us, and on top it is us too. Even though we have the choice and we know we should and ought to be able to do it, still we destroy it for our own sake. In this case we become our worst enemy. We give ourselves the blame i.e. I am not good enough, who do I think I am? I am unable, I am useless, I am worthless, I am a nobody, I can't do it, etc. Of course this negativity of energy is trying to destroy what we built, and might and most likely will lead to do so. We all like to aim high and be part of the high vibrations of life, each one of us. However, sometimes, even being aware, the consciousness is not able to make this vital choice.

When this scenario is repeating itself, meaning the dialogue between you and yourself is doing the same, blaming and putting yourself down in certain situations, here and there or even on a daily basis, I would say there is a pattern, a pattern that is repeating itself, a pattern which is coming from your family dynamic. Now you are asking, what is a family pattern? It is an attitude between family members that is led from one generation to the other.

Let's explain it further. I will try to explain it in a very simple way. We have a mum and a dad; they give us certain feelings from birth, even before we are born, until we reach a certain age and leave home. These certain feelings are going to follow us in life. Some feelings will be of love, support, help, courage, harmony, pride, etc. in a balanced dose or even over the top where there is no space for breathing and expanding; and some feelings will be of rejection, blaming, of being a failure, no recognition, being denied, shame, guilt, punishment etc. and sometimes we are alone, no parents and or no family at all, any kinds of traumas.

We know early on how we can 'play' the parents to get what is needed for us and also the parents know how to 'play' us so they will get what they need individually...

Actions are taken with certain conditions attached!

That is the dynamic between family members. When we do well we get love, when we misbehave, meaning when we are not doing what the parents want from us, we get rejection. And sometimes we have to find ways to survive. Our emotional wellbeing is led by the parents until we grow up and leave home. Subconsciously these behaviour patterns are rooted deeply into our personality. We build and put on layers from an early age, for our own survival and protection, not to be hurt and/ or not to be seen, etc. These behaviour patterns will lead, to a certain extent, our adult life and will attract similar situations that will put us into that same feeling that we know from home which is very familiar to us; we will attract relationships with partners, friends, colleagues – the pattern, the feeling that we know from home.

That is the relationship between mother and father, the relationship between the child and the parent.

We will attract people that way, either feeling great about ourselves or feeling not great about ourselves. Our parents, when they were young, had very similar experiences from their parents. This is why our parents are given exactly the same expression, passing it on to us... for us to carry on with the same pattern.

This generation family pattern is repeating itself over and over again, not even knowing that we do the same thing subconsciously because it is so deep rooted in us, almost unbreakable.

If you see that you always repeat the same pattern of being the enemy towards yourself in certain stages in your life, or even on a regular basis, perhaps daily, at this point I would highly recommend taking a step back with awareness and kindness. Please try to be open and honest with and in yourself. We all have these patterns that we repeat and repeat until it becomes knowledgeable and visible. Remember at the end we do have a choice. We always have a choice to make certain changes. In this case it is breaking the family pattern.

A healthy consciousness will guide you to make a choice. You can ask for help anytime in your life. Having the courage and being brave for asking to be helped is the first step of recognising the pattern. There are some great therapies available and there are just therapies available. Some therapies do solve the invisible, bring it out and work with it in a very positive, safe and active way, and some just move it from one side to the other.

Please be aware and do your research thoroughly or you can take my word – I highly recommend family constellation. That is an energy work with solid grounds and foundation that shows you your family pattern. It brings your 'why do I behave like this?' to having the opportunity of cutting the pattern off and healing your family tree, your past and your future. It is a beautiful work either in a group or one to one. There is no requirement to talk about yourself and express your inner dialogue. It is a high-frequency work, where you will see with clarity the 'why' and receive 'aha' moments that will lead to 'it makes sense' confirmation, forgiveness, compassion and gratitude. You will be left with a deep knowledge that everything is OK.

Your patterns are here for a reason.

It is magical ... no need to do anything with expressing, talking or even sharing. Just leave it and the energy is doing what is necessary. Trust and belief is vital in this process and in yourself, where layers of protection will peel off, slowly, step by step, which we all put on when we needed to survive. It is for our own survival. How, it doesn't really matter, it works – full stop! It is not your concern, it is the therapist who is in charge. Trust and believe is the motto! (If you need to know more please look up 'family constellation' on Google, there is a lot of information about it). You are changing the direction already; the pattern is faced and is turning into becoming your best friend.

d) Real Magic Is On Its Way

Yes, real magic is on its way.

This is another level of work on you and within you, from people who are here to help. People like you and me, to be able to meet the true self with a bit of work on this level of consciousness. The awareness will rise on a higher level of frequencies, where more clarity will surround you, and definitely you have a true friend with you... that is *you!*

We are living in a world where people are fast asleep, where pressure from the outside is growing, where confusion and insecurity is appearing in certain places on Mother Earth. We are surrounded and are living in a 'blaming' culture. If we are on the high level of frequencies, we are able **together** to build this wall of light and love, spread out awareness with a solid foundation – hmmm, what do you think?

One of my dreams or visions that happened a while ago and I would love to share with you is I saw an army of white dressed 'soldiers' all lined up, these 'soldiers' were my loved ones, my family, my friends and me, with golden arrows pointing to the opposite side that is black, slimy and sleepy; shooting across, shooting awareness and love to awaken them to that awareness of movement...

So imagine we all have access to that level of vibration – what might or will happen around us?

Working on that level of consciousness, a level that will bring a solid foundation, a good structure with simple rules where we can create and build our dream, our vision, our purpose that wants and needs to be

expressed and be visible to fulfil our fate, our destiny –
our own legacy!

On this path are some great gifts to be picked up...
trust and believe in yourself and your own process.

There is great help too. We just have to reach out, some amazing people are here to help and guide us so we can achieve whatever we want with much more clarity and definitely with much less family pattern baggage.

Please be aware that our family inheritance
can also be our blessings!

Without them we would not be here today and would not be able to break these patterns and bring this kind of awareness to other people – please, please remember that and be grateful! At the end, friend or not friend...

... you are your best friend or
you are your worst enemy...
... the choice lies in you – choose wisely!

CHAPTER THREE

Pain And Confusion
Is A Process

IT IS part of life. This is the time where we need to go into our depth and give ourselves the permission to do so. There are times on our journey where we are not doing well, not coping with ourselves at all. The connection is lost between reality and us. At the beginning of this uncomfortable feeling it is easy to avoid it and cover up, thinking, pretending that everything is fine, everything is OK, almost like, actually, putting a plaster on it and getting on with life. The wound doesn't heal, it is still open and 'annoyingly' in the way. Sometimes the pain does go away, just for a while, and it does come back in a different form. We can't really put a finger on it. It starts to grow and can become almost threatening. It keeps us awake at night, not breathing properly, tummy completely locked etc.

We all go through these kinds of experiences in our lives. We need to feel pain, a time for change is appearing, it is coming towards us. Something has to die to be born; something new is ready to enter our life. This process is painful and confusing and unfortunately it takes time.

These important times are:

- ❧ **for letting go the old habit**
- ❧ **for healing**
- ❧ **for facing the reality**
- ❧ **for uncovering some unexpected surprises**
- ❧ **for forming new habits**
- ❧ **for asking for help**
- ❧ **for approaching a different direction on our journey**

The help will come in different forms, shapes, people and events. When we start to face it, because we have had enough of suffering, the healing and transformation takes place. Of course it won't happen straight away or overnight, as I mentioned with the cycles before. Also this is one of the cycles where naturally our essence, our true self is ready to look into the depth of our own inner 'cellar', open finally the rusty door and walk into the darkness to face the shadows. It is scary and all kinds of fears or even monsters will appear.

These are our own shadows, our own monsters, and a part of ourselves. Life has both sides: good and bad, light and dark, black and white, yin and yang. We cannot exist without the other side. Also we have these two polarities in us that will seek to be recognised and embraced. By facing it, a bit like the story where the princess kisses the frog. Something ugly, threatening and demanding becomes something beautiful, strong and majestic... the frog transforms into a prince, the process of transformation begins.

So, by entering into our trust and belief system, and having the confidence that we started to build already, which is in and with us, our 'cellar' gets lightened up. This natural need is vital and very organic. By looking into these hidden 'shadows/pain' we are able finally to let go of the past, heal and transform. Each one of us in our unique way. Some need longer and some can face it straight away – actually there are no rules.

Pain is there so that the transformations can happen. By denying the pain, we cheat ourselves of transformation and taking the opportunity away. By accepting it the process of transformation can begin.

'For a tree's branches to reach to heaven, its roots must reach to hell.'

- Medieval alchemical dictum -

May I share with you my transformation? My father passed away when I was 21 years old. He was a very unhappy and lost spirit. When he was gone I felt relieved. There were no more arguments, no tears, no tension, no silent anger and discomfort at home.

Of course, with time this relieved feeling caught up with me and became quite uncomfortable, almost unbearable to deal with it. I could not cope anymore and asked for help. Actually I had this need to be rescued. I was almost praying, because I did not know what was happening with me and I did not like it.

At that time I was in a serious and comfortable relationship. We had a beautiful home and travelled to the most amazing places. I had my financial freedom to do exactly what I wanted to fulfil my desires. Still, inside I was lost and confused. My relationship broke; I stopped working, almost from one day to the other. I sold all my belongings, all my designer stuff and took my 'makeup' off... this was the time where I looked at myself and asked: Why **me**? The pain that I felt became finally visible. It was time to do something different.

I let my pain lead me, let go of everything and just became 'I'... Intuitive.

I found some coloured paints and brushes and went crazy – my inner artist was born. I loved the feeling of letting go and finding my inner peace by expressing this inner pain through painting. With this experience, tapping into familiar but still strange feelings, things started to happen from the outside. Help was coming in different forms, shapes, events and people. I really can't put it into words; something magical just started to happen in front of me:

- ❧ I had the urge to connect with nature, so I was cycling a lot, really a lot (also I sold my car and wanted a complete feeling of independence and freedom)

- ❧ I had the urge to express my inner fire, which was held back by my environment and circumstances, created by my family, and through dance and great help from shamanism workshops it came alive

- ❧ I had the urge to look inside and work on myself, so I discovered psychosynthesis and family constellation

- ❧ I had the urge for knowledge and reading different books, 'unusual' books, and guess what … books appeared from nowhere; psychological astrology was one of them and it became a big part of my life, and still is today

All these tools helped me to understand my family pattern in more detail and led to clarity, my father's sadness, his behaviour, the loss of his inner drive, which led to my sadness, to my behaviour and the loss of my inner drive… my actions and attractions. Step by step I looked into my shadows and took them out into the light. The healing took place naturally and painting became a big part of my life and of my healing process:

- ❧ without the pain my inner artist would not have come out and would not have been born

- ❧ without looking inside and facing my shadows, I would not have attracted astrology, psychosynthesis and family constellation

These painful moments were leading me to do something completely different, out of my comfort zone, and opened up something beautiful and magical that was ready to be born ... to become visible and to be shared with others.

a) Pain Leads To Transformation

Pain is a necessary part of our lives and it brings something out from the depth that will surprise each one of us. At the end of this dark, painful journey, where we thought we might go to die, there is a beautiful gift ready for us to be taken; it is almost like a reward for going through this painful journey and staying on this path, trusting and believing in our own process. It is a part of our authenticity, a part of our true self, our essence. We all have the opportunity to look inside and dig deep. Some earlier and some later in life, it depends when the universal cycles activate our being, our existence, as I mentioned in the first chapter. This cycle is about death and rebirth, like the story of the phoenix that comes out of the ashes. Do you know the story?

Let's tell you the story of the phoenix, simply described:

The phoenix is a mythical bird from Ancient Greek and Roman legends. Phoenix is associated with the sun and referred as a firebird, with feathers of gold and scarlet. This beautiful bird lives for many hundreds of years before it dies by setting itself on fire. It burns itself to create a new young phoenix that arises out of the ashes, it is reborn anew to live again. The meaning

of phoenix is one who has arisen from the flames,
has beaten all challenges and the hard times of life.
Therefore, phoenix symbolises rebirth from the ashes
of the past and it also represents the victory of life
over death.

Unfortunately, it is a painful experience and something that no one wants to go through, and very difficult to put into words. We all experience it and we all feel it differently. I have to say, it is part of life – please remember that! It makes us more who we really are, takes the layers off that we put on ourselves to survive when we were tiny, little, lost and alone... layers that were necessary to protect ourselves. The time brings us the opportunities to take these layers off and with our pain we can see and feel that is time to let go.

'There is no coming to consciousness without pain.'

- C.G. Jung -

b) Help And Support Designed By You

A structured help and support designed by you is necessary, almost essential to go through these experiences, something like a timetable that will make sure you do certain steps to stay close to yourself with kindness and compassion. It might be that you will start to have dreams, very profound dreams, or even feel restless and frustrated. Whatever it is, remember to be kind and loving towards yourself at these moments of stillness or restlessness and transformation.

CR A notebook, your journal to write and express these emotions, putting it down in your own words will bring an inner release, take away a bit of the tension; writing is connected with healing and letting go, out of your mind and body.

CR Regular connections with nature e.g. cycling, walking, running, whatever suits you, that you feel comfortable with it (make sure you do it daily constantly) – grounding will bring stability, a form of structure to move forward step by step.

CR Observing nature, recognising what is around you – trees, flowers, birds, sky, sun, moon etc. – it is your natural home, a part of life. It will bring you back into here and now.

CR Meditation, to find peace and connection to the true self, the inner source that will guide and support the steps which will lead to transforming the situation and you.

If you need more guidance on meditation, please go to Chapter 1, where the steps are explained in more detail.

To follow the timetable created by you will bring a good foundation for these emotions to be expressed. The universe with its cycles activating our movements, Mother Earth keeping us grounded and our true essence will make sure that we are achieving exactly what we are here for. Step by step, day by day... remember, it is a journey and it takes time to explore and discover something beautiful – **that is called 'I'.** So, please be patient, kind and loving towards yourself and have compassion at these moments in your life. Don't give up on yourself and don't be harsh on yourself; keep going and moving, step by step. Follow these rules regularly, appreciate and celebrate every little achievement.

When there are crises, the pains are accepted;
with this acceptance with time comes the recognition
that going through this experience has
been a necessary part of your growth
and unfoldment.
Hardship turns into wisdom.

Today, I make so many people happy with my art, touch their hearts, give so many parents an insight for their little ones with my 'map of heaven' (birth charts) and for me, whenever I feel pain, tension and discomfort, I get lost in my colours and my stars. This experience is priceless, thanks to my pain and confusion that gave me a tool for life, giving, sharing a gift for my family, friends, community – the world. I am very grateful for this part of my life and everyone has a gift inside to be given and to be shared with others; these experiences are really priceless and yes, thanks to pain and confusion, we are where we are.

c) A Story

So, we are all happy and excited about our newfound gift, the tool that we discovered of being more authentic the way we are. I thought so until another situation came along and took me down, like a roller coaster, to the depth of a different layer of feelings: meeting my partner's children and becoming a part of a family that is not my own.

I fell in love with my soul mate and it was an instant feeling from my side. It was actually love at first sight. My tummy was full of butterflies that I never experienced before, very special indeed. For him, I guess... that is another story! When I met his beautiful children for the first time, I thought, it will be OK. Of course, it was not OK. They pressed every button possible on my soul but also I assumed I was doing the same for them – pain and confusion from both sides. I did not understand where my role was. Was I girlfriend and mother? I am not their mother but somehow I thought I had to be their mother.

So, instead of becoming something or someone, I went inside and found my answers. Getting in touch with my rituals (remember Chapter 1), that helped me through these difficult times, being committed and focused gave me a good base for understanding their true needs. These little souls were coming from a divorce that was very painful, losing Mummy and Daddy being together. Their 'perfect' world fell apart and not even having the understanding of what really happened. It was very traumatic for the whole family to go through this difficult separation.

I realised that I didn't want to be their mother; they have their mummy and I am not their stepmother either. (The word stepmother has a bitter taste and is known in stories to be difficult and rigid; energy wise it does not resonate with me!) What these little ones really needed was love without any conditions, support, guidance, some kind of stability, safety and friendship. They didn't need a competition between two women fighting over them or even thinking that Daddy's girlfriend will be taking Daddy away from them. I started to understand that by being their friend they might see that I am not a threat to them.

It was not easy to go through this pain and confusion. I knew what I needed to do and wanted to do; I became their friend and gave them enough space for their healing, unconditional love and never expected anything back. I left them to decide if they needed or wanted me. I never said anything bad or negative about their mother, even when there were some difficulties and great challenges. In the end she is their mother and has to be respected as the mother. When my children were born I was still there for them, still their friend for their needs and support. Of course, the energy changed naturally around us as a family. However, the foundation stayed the same, solid and grounded.

As you can see, there are two scenarios with pain and confusion. The little ones experienced it very early in their lives and went through their own pain of separation and losing the family unit. The time brought confusion and even more pain. With my awareness from my previous experiences I used all these rituals that I mentioned before and helped them to their own healing. The second scene is me, myself experiencing pain and confusion on another level: where and what is my role in this situation? Having a partner with young children brings interesting challenges to the relationship. I went to my rituals and stayed focused, knowing that these little steps would help my new family and me. My partner was introduced to family constellation to gain the awareness and to have an understanding about the bigger picture.

Experiences that bring out our authenticity, as I said before, are priceless. Without my experience, my pain and confusion, in the first place I would not be able to help these little ones and give them unconditional love without expecting anything back. I was the adult and they were allowed to be the children. I am grateful to have these beautiful children in my life, and they are part of my life. And a 'thank you' to their mother for giving birth, welcoming these two beautiful spirits.

You never know what life will bring to you. There is no need to worry. It will come exactly the way you need to experience it... and these life experiences will take the layers off to release your authenticity, being yourself and sharing your gift with others unconditionally... *your unique way.*

> *'Your pain is but the breaking of the shell*
> *that encloses your understanding.'*
>
> *- Kahlil Gibran -*

View at *www.jasminkahansson.com*

I AM LIFE

CHAPTER FOUR

There Is A Reason That You Are In This Situation

YES, WE do choose certain situations for ourselves to learn from it. There are important lessons here and now to look at and try to make sense from it. What we go through in our lives and what we feel inside will be mirrored from the outside. It is a bit like a real mirror is shown to us. With awareness and clarity we can see what the mirror is presenting. It is our choice to look at it or to turn away. This presenting from the outside through these mirrors will come in different shapes and forms, people and events.

(The topic 'mirror' is explained in more detail in Chapter 6 – We Are All A Mirror For Each Other. No jumping forward, stay in this natural flow of the chapters!)

When we look very closely we can see what moves in front of us:

- **if we looked away 'yesterday'**
- **if we look away 'today'**

- **it will come back 'tomorrow' in a different form, different colours... from time to time!**

These situations that are displayed for ourselves are an amazing opportunity for our growth, for opening up and making sure that we become who we really are, our authentic self. However, it is a good start to see what the mirror is presenting 'today'. This is exactly what is mirroring from the outside. There are certain pictures presented to us that we like to ignore sometimes. We can take a closer look and embrace the situation. We have parts in ourselves that need to come out and be looked at.

Each part has its own time to be playing, recognised and appreciated in certain situations, certain topics i.e. relationships, family, becoming a parent, value and self-worth, finances, friendship, work, creativity, having fun, higher education, leading the self and others, health, our community and the world.

It is important to face it and learn from it. If we face it now and take a closer look, then it is done and we can move forward. The situation is just a reminder, a bit like double-checking, to see if we are on the right path or missed the turning.

Subconscious questions might be coming on the surface:

- **Is this where I am meant to go, walk, run, climb, rest, enjoy, cry, suffer, play etc.?**

- Are these people around me the people that I like, want, need for my climb to the next level of myself?

- Are these people leading me?

- Are these people keeping me down or even holding me back?

- Are these people encouraging me?

- Are these people draining me?

- Are these people supporting me?

- Are these people inspiring me?

- Are these people adding quality to my life?

These questions and more are always around us and we can give answers to them. Yes, by being really honest we can answer them with pride or sadness:

- Is this part of my life?

- Do I want to be in this part of my life?

- How long do I want to be in this part of my life?

Yes, we form, design and create our future. Yes, we can make changes and do something completely different.

Courage, taking risks and turning away from habits will provide and build a new path.

a) Clarity Takes Time

It will not happen today or tomorrow. It takes a while until this situation is looked at properly, weighing it up and making a decision: Is this where I want to be or not? It is very important to ask questions over and over again to get the exact answer – observe, look and listen! Little signs will appear to form the answer. Little appearances from nowhere will come out and lead or show where to turn. We don't know what is around the corner. As I mentioned before, in Chapter 2, 'trust and believe'. These words have to be with us all the time. Breathe in and breathe out! Again, trust and believe in these unique steps. We know that it is not easy. There will be moments where everything is sunshine and we feel strong, that kind of strength that we can move mountains. There will be moments where the whole world is falling down on to our shoulders. That is OK too.

The moments where the sun shines on us is when we are in connection with ourselves and know exactly that we are moving into our unique purpose, our unique goal. And then there are moments where we have to slow down and feel the heaviness so we know that these steps are important to make sure to be grounded and not to fly away into the sun and just dream and dream and dream. Only by doing steps in here and now we can and will manifest these insights. We need these steps, action steps. Action is where things do happen...

Without planting a seed into the soul – action;
there is no flower – manifestation.

b) Each Approach Is Different

As we know, we are all individual in our approaches, some of us go 'Speedy Gonzales', some of us need time to digest emotionally, and some of us need to be very sure and certain of these steps, and some of us need things to be perfect. There is no right or wrong! It is our personality, our own makeup, how we do steps of action in life.

Like the elements of Mother Earth – fire, earth, air and water:

- Fire/straightforward
- Earth/grounded
- Air/thoughtful with 101 ideas
- Water/going with the flow… (simply described!)

We are part of this, part of this amazing energy around us and in us. Our instinct, our gut feeling is true, very true for all of us. Follow your gut feeling and try to learn about this amazing instinct that you have already in you. It tells you exactly what has to be done. This unique feeling is the guidance and protection wherever you go and move towards your purpose, your goal. There are times that we like to worry and look into pain as long as possible. There are times that we like to blame others for certain actions. That is OK… however, for moving forward look into these mirrors around you. Don't forget, the mirrors are showing you all the time, every time wherever you go and where you are at the moment in your life. Actually it is all in your hands.

c) Concentrate On Solutions

*If we all could concentrate on 20% worries
and 80% solutions,*

it would make our life much easier.

Concentrate on solutions, where you start to ask certain questions, it will lead you away from worries. Your mind will be occupied to find and get the solutions much more quickly, to solve the situation in front of you. Also, if you remember, I mentioned in Chapter 2 that words have power, either positive or negative. It is your choice! Be aware that it takes time to make changes. Only one step, the first step, towards making a change is by simply looking around and looking into the mirror, so please be kind to yourself! It is an amazing achievement already to see where you are now at this moment.

d) Trust In Intuition

There was a time in my life where exactly that happened, where I asked myself, hmmm, what does this mean? My mirror did not fit anymore, people around me did not fit my vision anymore, my work did not fit my desires anymore... there were certain steps to make, one step towards change. I took these certain steps and one of them was my decision to visit my friend in England. I did not know why, I followed my gut feeling, trusted and believed that this was the right choice. And guess what! I met my husband to be, almost on day one. Of course, he did not know that. I had this incredible feeling that **he** would be the father of my children. That **he** is the one. How stupid, I thought. There is no such feeling really! Somehow, out of the blue, a job came towards me, meaning I asked for a job in a lovely cute old English café called Wishing Well. They offered me a place to work. My English at that time was very weak but I was a keen learner. At that time I was single and free. I took this opportunity, locked my flat in Vienna and stayed in England for a while. I learned the language and tried to make myself visible to this 'husband to be'. He did not see me and was not interested in me at all. I did not give up. There was this incredible instinct that I had to move forward and make sure that he would meet me soon. I put all my courage into this situation, trusted and believed that something would happen. That was 20 years ago... yes, I followed my gut feeling and did not give up. We are married and have beautiful children.

There was a reason that I came to England, there was a reason that I changed my job, my friends and moved away to another country. My friends thought I was crazy and they did not understand what I was doing. Even I could not explain it. I just followed my instinct, step by step, and arrived where I needed to be for that moment. There is a reason why we choose certain situations in our lives; for me, one of them was to meet my husband, my soul mate, the father of my children and the start of a new chapter.

Being consciously aware as much as possible,
as much as you can be in here and now
your instinct, your gut feeling will become reality.

I would like to share one of my favourite poems that I found many, many years ago. Unfortunately I don't know who the author is. It is still with me today, sometimes I put it up to be seen and sometimes it is just in my notebook... my reason.

REASON

People come into your life for a Reason, a Season or a Lifetime. When you know which one it is for a person, you will know what to do for that person.

When someone is in your life for a Reason, it is usually to meet a need you have expressed. They have come to assist you through a difficulty, to provide you with guidance and support, to aid you physically, emotionally or spiritually. They are there for the reason you need them to be.

Then, without any wrongdoing on your part or at an inconvenient time, this person will say or do something to bring the relationship to an end. Sometimes they die. Sometimes they walk away. Sometimes they act up and force you to take a stand. What we must realise is that our need has been met, our desire fulfilled, their work is done.

The prayer you sent up has been answered, and now it is time to move on.

Some people come into your life for a Season, because your turn has come to share, grow or learn. They bring you an experience of peace or make you laugh. They may teach you something you have never done. They usually give you an unbelievable amount of joy.

Believe it! It is real! But only for a Season!

Lifetime *relationships teach you lifetime lessons, things you must build upon in order to have a solid emotional foundation. Your job is to accept the lesson, love the person and put what you have learned to use in all other relationships and areas of your life. It is said that love is blind but friendship is clairvoyant.*

Thank you for being a part of my life.

A special thank you to the person who put this beautiful poem out for sharing and inspiring.

I AM LIFE

CHAPTER FIVE

Only You Can
Unleash Yourself

IS IT easy or is it scary to find out what is underneath your self? Hmmm, what do you think? Imagine you are amazing, worthy, beautiful, special, unique, fantastic, brilliant, only one of you here on Mother Earth... of course we all are in our own ways amazing, worthy, beautiful, special, unique, fantastic, brilliant! However, it is quite scary to open up this amazing self and put it out there – open up this awesome 'I' and stand tall and say YES! Unfortunately, there are people out there who are saying completely different things about us and sometimes it starts from our parents, when we were little or/and even today... not being good enough, who do you think you are, how dare you think you are different, don't stand out, there is not enough money, be quiet 'to be seen but not heard', don't say what you think, you are not worth it... the list is long. I am sure most of us have a sentence, a 'believing system', which brings these barriers and makes sure we are not better than the others around us and we don't stand out.

We do all dream and wish we could be this or that. Our dreams can be colourful and full of imagination, either during the day or when we go to sleep or even the whole day. We can see ourselves doing some amazing stuff, being the star of 'today and tomorrow', being recognised, bringing something unique, doing something special. However, the doubt that is in us can be quite difficult to overcome. Perhaps there are some friends, family members, neighbours and/or colleagues – 'the people' would talk and point a finger towards us. Let's forget about these 'people' and focus on you. We really don't care what others think about us!

You might be the one who will inspire them one day and guide them to their uniqueness and transformation – hmmm, that sounds much better!

a) The Star

For now it is all about YOU!

Let's pretend, let's imagine **you are that star,** you are exactly that person that you imagine – you are beautiful and perfect, full of life and light, vitality and optimism just pours out of you. Your movements are balanced and in harmony. You express joy in every breath and you are feeling fulfilled in every part of your body. A sense of serenity is shining through you. You live in this amazing wonderful place surrounded by the most beautiful nature of smell and sound and have exactly what you always dreamed of, you are on top of the world – close your eyes for a moment and see your imagination, your awesome picture. Breathe in and breathe out, enjoy the moment of **being that star**... Can you handle yourself knowing **you are the star**, can you deal with this surrounding of people saying how amazing you are, how beautiful you are and how special you are?

Hmmm, that is the question – it might be quite overwhelming to be put up so high and expect to be someone who you are not yet. One day we will get to become our own star and this one day can be today or tomorrow, or never. It is really up to you.

Whatever you went through in your childhood, young adulthood, in your life so far, it is part of you. It makes you special and unique:

- ❧ **with doubts and craziness**
- ❧ **with support and help**
- ❧ **with struggle and 'hunger'**
- ❧ **with loneliness and pain**
- ❧ **with love and abundance**

It all belongs to you and is somewhere deep inside you. You can dream of the past, you can dream of the future, but somehow you need to be present and embrace everything that is here in front of you.

b) True Love

True love comes only from you:

- **loving you the way you are and making sure there is plenty of it**
- **acceptance, where you are today and being grateful for your journey so far**
- **being your own best friend is where security and safety will arise**
- **kindness and inner value will bring confidence in your own feelings**
- **being aware that words are used to encourage your steps on your journey**
- **your language that you use on a regular basis is becoming part of your expression to others**

These 'little' actions sound so simple, but for most of us it is quite difficult. Becoming who we are we have to start to look inside first. There is no way to imagine all these amazing things on the outside and not doing anything inside. First we need to climb the mountain so we can stand on the top of this mountain, our mountain, chosen by us. Without doing these steps we cannot be there. Without finding out who we really are we cannot be **the star** to shine bright and strong.

'We fear our highest possibilities. We are generally afraid to become that which we can glimpse in our most perfect moments, under conditions of great courage.

*We enjoy and even thrill to godlike possibilities we
see in ourselves in such peak moments. And yet
we simultaneously shiver with weakness, awe, and
fear before these very same possibilities.'*

- A Maslow -

So, what has to be done is always in your hands. Either dream big and just dream or start to look into the depth and finally move into a direction, to your mountain. Start to meet parts of yourself and take opportunities that come your way. Being brave enough to open up doors and look inside, see the possibilities that are out there. Even having doubts and being judged by others, still, step by step, moving in a direction. Who knows what you might meet out there, what kind of person is going to be unleashed and what kind of gift you are carrying in yourself ?

This special gift that we all have, each one of us, is unique and individual and it can be discovered and unleashed... only by us. It is a journey and it takes time – full stop!

Like the nature on Mother Earth, the natural cycles – if we observe the caterpillar that becomes a beautiful butterfly, the rose that is opening one petal after the other to show the full beauty and the perfume that comes with it. We are all linked together by these cosmic rules of the universe that we are able to unleash our beauty, our unique gift and give it to the world. Our blueprint, the DNA, its natural expression is waiting to be fully recognised. It is up to us to do what has to be done. I would say embrace and get on with it... in the end we are only humans and not angels! We are humans on Mother Earth with the connection to the higher frequencies of dreams and visions to be reminded of. Remember the rituals on a daily basis that will lead to breaking the habits and making the change possible – yes, there is some work involved... so...

... action, grounding and staying focused on your self
to fulfil your destiny, your purpose,
the authenticity of 'I'.

I AM LIFE

CHAPTER SIX

We Are All A Mirror For Each Other

'Human relations are for self-revelation, not self-gratification.

People, especially true friends, are mirrors in which we begin to discover ourselves.'

- H.F. Weekley -

On our journey we meet people, all kinds of people. Some we like and they become friends, some we do not like ... either they walk away or we walk away. All of them are here actually for us, for our realisation, but also we are here for others, showing them where they are. A bit like a mirror, showing us where we are and what we are at the moment or even become what we see in others one day. The inside 'I' is attracting from the outside to show us how far we have travelled inside.

Also checking:

- **Is this is important to me?**
- **Is this where I want to be?**

It is highlighting who we are at the moment. It is really helpful if it can be seen with awareness and acknowledged with clarity 'what is in front of me'. It is a bit like a checklist:

- **Is this still my dream?**
- **Does this fit my dream?**
- **Is this leading to achieving my dream?**
- **Am I out of my senses?**
- **Am I happy in this situation i.e. at work, in my relationship, at home, in my environment etc.?**
- **Do I feel fulfilled and content?**
- **Who are these people around me?**
- **Are they my true friends?**
- **Are they adding to my life and to my growth?**
- **Or are they using my kindness and filling their ego?**

The list can be quite long, depending on how big our dream is.

a) Discomfort Or Fulfilment

Is it a feeling of discomfort or fulfilment? A mirror from the outside is a good guidance and can be used anytime. We all go through different phases on our journey and of course we have different mirrors to look at. Sometimes we don't want to or even can't because we are:

- busy climbing
- building a nest/home
- building our own business
- caring and looking after loved ones
- needing a rest, or even
- sleeping for a while to get our inner battery recharged
- having our beauty sleep
- in general occupied with life at this very moment!

At these important times, at these phases, it is good to see:

- who is around us?
- where is their journey taking them?
- do we want to be part of their journey?
- do we need to be on our own journey?

A good indicator for our realisation is the question:

Is this where I want to be or what I want to be surrounded by?

When you find a little moment, a bit of breathing time and have the time to observe, you might be surprised how much has changed around you. The time is going very fast, especially when you are busy building the foundation of your life or a new chapter in your life. When you finally have the mirror in front of you, holding it really straight and facing the reality with a clear mind – **yes**, that is **me...** Look at yourself, really look at you, straight in your eyes, and breathe in and breathe out, keep your head straight and stay in that moment.

What do you see? Look at:

- **your posture: how do you stand, where are your shoulders?**
- **your eyes: do they sparkle or look empty?**
- **your smile: which direction are your lips pointing – up or down?**
- **your hair: is it shiny or dull?**

What clothes do your wear? Are they:

- **colourful**
- **smart**
- **casual**
- **clean**
- **stylish**
- **rough**
- **messy**
- **dirty**
- **smelly**

How is your voice? Is it:

- **happy**
- **sad**
- **quiet**

- strong
- loud
- confident

Whatever you see in front of you, recognise every part of you and honour yourself, this is **you** at the moment. Don't forget **you** are beautiful, special and unique. Being grateful for what you achieved so far, being in here and now. Celebrate yourself and look back at your past, where you came from, and see what the future, your future will bring and one day deliver. Focus on here and now:

- **What is important for you now?**
- **Are there any changes to make?**
- **Does your dream fit the surroundings today?**
- **Is your dream on paper so it can be manifested in a way that suits you?**

b) Your Dream Board

Creating a dream board for yourself is a great exercise to be reminded where you wish:

- **to go**
- **to be**
- **to bring and share to the world**

What is a dream board? you might ask. A dream board is where you capture your dream, your vision. By putting it on paper it will start to manifest and become reality.

I will give you some guidance on how you can make your own dream board. Remember to be creative and use your own imagination, anything is possible and there are no rules, go with the flow. Exciting time... let's start and have some fun!

It can be done at the beginning of a new year, a new chapter – any time that suits you. You can create this dream board alone, with friends or family. Find a moment, a day, a time that suits you. Find a place where you feel comfortable and have unlimited time, no pressure. Make sure the mobile phone is off, no interruption from the outside. You will need scissors, old/new magazines, newspapers, pens (colours in every shade), glue, and A3 paper or even bigger-size paper. Anything really that you can find at home. Create a space with candles, play soothing music e.g. meditation, instrumental, classical etc. It can be on the floor, on the table or even outside.

Prepare yourself with a little meditation before you start. Close your eyes and breathe in and out a few times. Let go of your daily thoughts, worries, tasks etc. and be in this moment. You will start to feel relaxed. Imagine your dream, feel your dream, focus on your dream and go with the flow. Your spirit, your true essence will guide you to your inner source, trust and believe in yourself. You will feel a beautiful energy around you. It is quite magical... **imagine** and go wild with it... open your eyes and start creating your dream on the paper.

Please don't worry if you don't see anything and there are no pictures.

Stay in this feeling, a feeling of bliss and relaxation and see what comes your way. Go with the flow and just enjoy the process. Cut out what comes towards you, pictures of nature, people etc., write words down or cut them out, paint or draw – there are no rules. We are all unique and we all have our own special dreams. Each dream is different and unique, perfect the way in which we see it. Please don't compare and there is no competition.

When you are finished, after an hour, a few hours or the whole day, have a look at your creation, your dream. Share it with family, friends or just with yourself, depends on who is with you. Reflect on what you put on the paper – does it make you feel excited, does it feel overwhelming? Whatever you feel it is OK. Recognise it and thank yourself. Now find a spot where you want to see your dream, your dream board creation, every day. This is where the manifestation comes in. Keep it for a year or as long as you need to. Let it become a ritual that you look at your dream every day at least twice and visualise it. You will be surprised when one day it becomes true, manifestation in reality.

I have used this exercise since my twenties and I love it. This is a way in which I visualise myself, become my own creator of my dreams. Through this exercise I attracted my soul mate into my life, my wonderful husband of 20 years. This is the way in which I visualised the birth of my beautiful children. Sometimes I need more time for my dream to be manifested and sometimes it takes less. It doesn't matter when and where. I needed to grow at the same time as my dream needed to be manifested. I need to be strong, confident, so that my real self is able to attract these dreams and manifest them. If my steps, actions, are not put in place nothing is going to happen, it would be just a fantasy. My dream boards are always placed in my bedroom next to me. When I wake up I see my dream board – clear, colourful and vibrant – and when I go to sleep the last picture in my mind is my dream board.

I am grateful for every little sign that is shown to me on the path to achieving my dream. This habit has been with me for many years. Of course with family things do change. However, this is an exercise that is part of my family too. Today, we as a family do our dream boards together. Usually, we like to do it at the beginning of the New Year... New Year, new beginning, new chapter, new opportunities etc. It is a special time for all of us as a family and also it brings the children awareness that everything, anything is possible. Everything that we wish for can and will come true.

Magic does happen... where focus goes, energy flows!

Don't forget to do what has to be done to achieve your dreams. The steps still come from you, the action has to be taken by you only. People and events will enter your sphere to help you to achieve your dreams. You make sure that you check regularly by holding the mirror towards you and look properly with clarity and awareness: what can I see? Honour it and be honest to yourself. You are your own best friend at the end and you can give yourself the love, and plenty of it, as I mentioned in Chapter 4. Enjoy the ride, your journey of achieving your dream – you will become the master of your creation of your destiny.

Look at yourself in the mirror, your own mirror, and ask yourself, really ask with conscious, certainty and love:

> *What do I want to do every day for the rest of my life?*
> *What do I want to achieve every day for the rest of my life?*

How does it make you feel – interesting isn't it?! I leave the answer with you, yourself and your feelings.

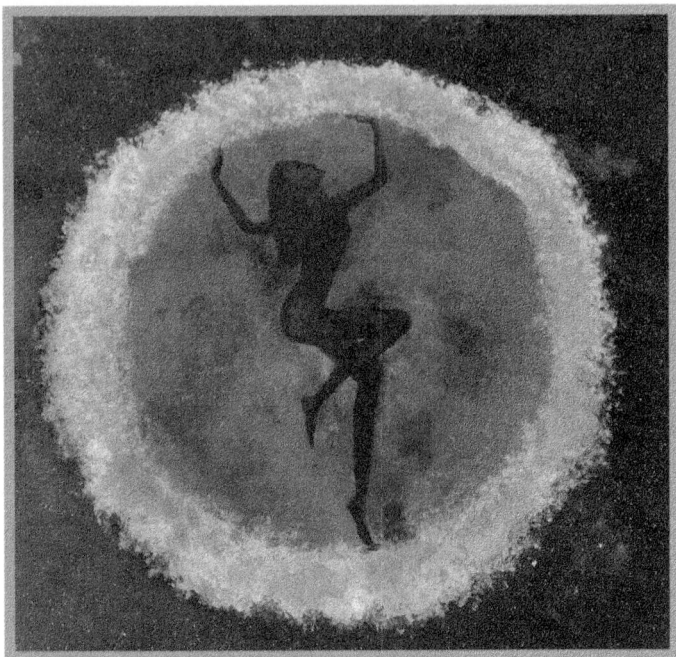

View at *www.jasminkahansson.com*

I AM LIFE

CHAPTER SEVEN

The Truth Is That You Have Everything In Yourself That You Need and Want

YES, YOU do, believe it or not – all you need is within yourself already. When asking the right questions the answers and help will come in different shapes and forms. The answer will be exactly what you need for here and now. However, it is the quality of asking the questions – a different form of questions. If we go by, if you remember at the beginning of the book, 'why always me?' the answer will be a 'blame' answer! 'I can't do it, I failed again, I don't have enough time, I am not good enough, he/she is not listening, he/she doesn't understand me' etc. I guess you know what I mean. We start to blame the situation or other people. Hmmm, and we are definitely not happy and fulfilled! So, that question 'why me?' is a no-no way! We are not achieving anything on this road.

Only you are responsible for your actions,
not the others.

There is really no one to blame. Having an under-standing **and** recognising that sometimes to achieve something 'big' that is out of reach at the moment, or where a lot of action is needed/required, is difficult, and perhaps it does make us feel drained and lost, tired and fed up. At these times we like to become lazy and rely on others. It is OK! Let's do something different. The something different could be to ask different questions so we can receive different answers that will help us to move further and **not** to slow us down or even stop us. Different answers can wake us up and we can feel ex-cited again. The inner source is activated and ready to give. The inner source is our essence, our own language that we understand very well, it resonates with us.

That is a great start to become balanced again, feel harmonised and energised. Almost like the inner battery is recharged and ready to be full on – used well! It is time to train ourselves for a clear mind. First look around… what is around you? We talked about the mirror in Chapter 6, what does the mirror show you?

- ◌ **Look at your home, your lifestyle, your relationship – is it messy?!**

- ◌ **How are your structures, your rules around you – hmmm, you might think… boring, and say I don't like structures; actually structures and rules lead to a firm and strong foundation ready to build a home, your own temple in all areas in your life.**

How are you looking after yourself? With kindness and being loving and caring towards yourself will lead to harmony and optimism.

If we are stressed, as we all know, we don't breathe; we are out of our body and mind and the emotions take over. Not being in control of our emotions, we start to behave a bit like 'little ones', blaming others! We don't want that, of course. So, step by step we make sure the situation is going to change, little by little. Remember it takes time! Question by question and the answers will lead to our source, where we connect and gain our power and get our strength back – a bit like being reminded that we are living and we need certain things to do so... for being alive. One of them is to be in touch with our inner source and our self.

I will share another ritual with you that I use regularly. As you can see, I do have quite a few rituals and I love them all! They have been part of my life for many years. So, all these little steps will lead to your destiny that you created already in yourself. It is on your dream board that you see every day. Your reminder is to stay focused and true to your dream, a minute here and a minute there! The other one is 'The Questions', profound questions from one of my heroes Tony Robbins. I changed only two things – the layout and the background for my own use ('Blue Cow' on canvas printed 80mm x 100mm).

Just a quick explanation of 'Blue Cow': what does 'Blue Cow' mean? you might ask! Blue Cow is the symbol for being different, pushing boundaries and following the inner gut feeling.

Let's tell you the story of the Blue Cow. There is a herd of brown cows moving from one corner of the field to the other, nicely fenced in. Here comes the blue cow and wants to explore more than being fenced in a field. She goes to the brown cows and says, 'I am going to the moon.' The brown cows say, 'You can't do that.' The blue cow doesn't listen. She follows her gut feeling, leaves the herd and goes on an adventure. On the road of adventure she is alone, however it brings her great experiences and growth in herself.

It is not easy to break out of comfort, habits and from people that bring rigidness, represented by the brown cows. There was a children's series on BBC many years ago, *The Blue Cow*, a fantastic message for the little ones.

So let's go back to our questions.

a) The Questions

The profound questions for the morning and evening:

Here we go! Let's start with the morning: these questions start with a big **'Good morning!'** (even use your name) before you get out of bed. Ask these questions every morning and something magical will happen. Your consciousness changes, you become lighter in yourself. It is just a beautiful feeling... it comes from the inside and is sooooo pure and clear. I can only say try it yourself and you will experience something very special!

Morning Power Questions

Questions you can ask yourself every morning to create an empowering focus:

1. What am I happy about in my life now?

What about that makes me happy?
How does that make me feel?

2. What am I excited about in my life now?

What about that makes me excited?
How does that make me feel?

3. What am I proud about in my life now?

What about that makes me proud?
How does that make me feel?

4. What am I grateful about in my life now?

What about that makes me grateful?
How does that make me feel?

5. What am I enjoying most in my life right now?

What about that do I enjoy?
How does that make me feel good?

6. What am I committed to in my life now?

What about that makes me committed?
How does that make me feel?

7. Who do I love? Who loves me?

What about that makes me loving?
How does that make me feel?

'Where focus goes energy flows.'

And now questions for the evening:

Evening Power Questions
Questions you can ask yourself every
evening to create an empowering focus:

1. What have I given today?
   In what ways have I been a giver today?

2. What did I learn today?

3. How has today added to the quality of my life?
   How can I use today as an investment in my future?

'Unleash the power within'... where the
impossible becomes possible...
... remember everyone has a unique gift and
purpose in life!

Here is the same – before you close your eyes you say
'Good night' to yourself and feel gratefulness for your
achievements today. Reflect!

If you need more answers please ask questions in
that kind of form. You will get the answers that you
need. They are true and real. Guess what, these answers
deliver – exactly what you need here and now! Your
sleep will be peaceful and you will wake up relaxed,
energised and ready for your new day!

How exciting is it being in charge of yourself and
your own destiny?! No one is interfering and telling you
where to go and what to do, no one. It is only you, you

and your rituals, being and staying focused as much as possible on a regular basis. These are your new habits. You know your path, you know your steps and only you are in charge. Whatever you meet or/and attract on the way is part of your dream – to become what you want and need to become. Don't forget it will take time. Just to mention again, and give you a reminder, as in Chapter 1, cycles approach us in ways that show from the outside that there is a need for change. Some cycles take a long time to go through an issue, a topic that is important to you and for you. We need to grow with it and learn from it as is given to us.

Life is full of colours and so is your truth. However, you can see the truth or you don't want to see the truth. It comes in all shades of colours, and sometimes also in black and white. When you miss it once or twice it will come back and knock on the door again and again. It is up to you to open the door and embrace it or fight it. Whatever you choose or take on either as a challenge or as an opportunity. Again, it is up to you. The truth is just the truth – sometimes it is colourful and sometimes it can be black and white.

b) A Profound Story

My daughter told me an interesting story that I would like to share with you. It is not everyone's cup of tea – for me it makes sense and it is beautifully put together. Let's take you to somewhere even more cosmic... out of space or into space! I leave this with you – have an open mind and try to see it from a different perspective.

The Egg

by Andy Weir

You were on your way home when you died.

It was a car accident. Nothing particularly remarkable, but fatal nonetheless. You left behind a wife and two children. It was a painless death. The EMTs tried their best to save you, but to no avail. Your body was so utterly shattered you were better off, trust me.

And that's when you met me.

"What... what happened?" you asked. "Where am I?"

"You died," I said, matter-of-factly. No point in mincing words.

"There was a... a truck and it was skidding..."

"Yup," I said.

"I... I died?"

"Yup. But don't feel bad about it. Everyone dies," I said.

You looked around. There was nothingness. Just you and me.

"What is this place?" you asked. "Is this the afterlife?"

"More or less," I said.

"Are you God?" you asked.

"Yup," I replied. "I'm God."

"My kids... my wife," you said.

"What about them?"

"Will they be all right?"

"That's what I like to see," I said. "You just died and your main concern is for your family. That's good stuff right there."

You looked at me with fascination. To you, I didn't look like God. I just looked like some man. Or possibly a woman. Some vague authority figure, maybe. More of a grammar school teacher than the Almighty.

"Don't worry," I said. "They'll be fine. Your kids will remember you as perfect in every way. They didn't have time to grow contempt for you. Your wife will cry on the outside, but will be secretly relieved. To be fair, your marriage was falling apart. If it's any consolation, she'll feel very guilty for feeling relieved."

"Oh," you said. "So what happens now? Do I go to heaven or hell or something?"

"Neither," I said. "You'll be reincarnated."

"Ah," you said. "So the Hindus were right."

"All religions are right in their own way," I said. "Walk with me."

You followed along as we strode through the void. "Where are we going?"

"Nowhere in particular," I said. "It's just nice to walk while we talk."

"So what's the point, then?" you asked. "When I get reborn, I'll just be a blank slate, right? A baby. So all my experiences and everything I did in this life won't matter."

"Not so!" I said. "You have within you all the knowledge and experiences of all your past lives. You just don't remember them right now."

I stopped walking and took you by the shoulders. "Your soul is more magnificent, beautiful, and gigantic than you can possibly imagine. A human mind can only contain a tiny fraction of what you are. It's like sticking your finger in a glass of water to see if it's hot or cold. You put a tiny part of yourself into the vessel, and when you bring it back out, you've gained all the experiences it had."

"You've been in a human for the last 48 years, so you haven't stretched out yet and felt the rest of your immense consciousness. If we hung out here for long enough, you'd start remembering everything. But there's no point to doing that between each life."

"How many times have I been reincarnated, then?"

"Oh lots. Lots and lots. And into lots of different lives," I said. "This time around, you'll be a Chinese peasant girl in 540 AD."

"Wait, what?" you stammered. "You're sending me back in time?"

"Well, I guess technically. Time, as you know it, only exists in your universe. Things are different where I come from."

"Where you come from?" you said.

"Oh sure," I explained. "I come from somewhere. Somewhere else. And there are others like me. I know you'll want to know what it's like there, but honestly you wouldn't understand."

"Oh," you said, a little let down. "But wait. If I get reincarnated to other places in time, I could have interacted with myself at some point."

"Sure. Happens all the time. And with both lives only aware of their own lifespan you don't even know it's happening."

"So what's the point of it all?"

"Seriously?" I asked. "Seriously? You're asking me for the meaning of life? Isn't that a little stereotypical?"

"Well it's a reasonable question," you persisted.

I looked you in the eye. "The meaning of life, the reason I made this whole universe, is for you to mature."

"You mean mankind? You want us to mature?"

"No, just you. I made this whole universe for you. With each new life you grow and mature and become a larger and greater intellect."

"Just me? What about everyone else?"

"There is no one else," I said. "In this universe, there's just you and me."

You stared blankly at me. "But all the people on earth…"

"All you. Different incarnations of you."

"Wait. I'm *everyone*!?"

"Now you're getting it," I said, with a congratulatory slap on the back.

"I'm every human being who ever lived?"

"Or who will ever live, yes."

"I'm Abraham Lincoln?"

"And you're John Wilkes Booth, too," I added.

"I'm Hitler?" you said, appalled.

"And you're the millions he killed."

"I'm Jesus?"

"And you're everyone who followed him."

You fell silent.

"Every time you victimised someone," I said, "you were victimising yourself. Every act of kindness you've done, you've done to yourself. Every happy and sad moment ever experienced by any human was, or will be, experienced by you."

You thought for a long time.

"Why?" you asked me. "Why do all this?"

"Because someday you will become like me. Because that's what you are. You're one of my kind. You're my child."

"Whoa," you said, incredulous. "You mean I'm a god?"

"No. Not yet. You're a foetus. You're still growing. Once you've lived every human life throughout all time, you will have grown enough to be born."

"So the whole universe," you said, "it's just…"

"An egg." I answered. "Now it's time for you to move on to your next life."

And I sent you on your way.

I guess it will take you into a different direction. It is an interesting approach to our existence of our being. I am sure it will bring some discussions on the table.

For me… I love it!

I AM LIFE

CHAPTER EIGHT

It Is Never Too Late,
The Time Is Always Right For You

WE ARE our own captains. We are in charge of our sails just waiting for the wind to take us from A to B. We are responsible for our route, meaning having an idea and knowing where we want to go. Sometimes, however, nature – the wind, a big storm, high waves etc. – will take us somewhere else, completely to the opposite, where we are not prepared at all. However, our tools that we shaped and formed will take care of these challenges. But sometimes there is no wind, no movement, only stillness. Mist comes in and there is no direction and no guidance and definitely no compass! With the mist comes the 'waiting' time. This 'waiting' time brings an energy of stillness that approaches us and will lead to:

ᘓ **a time for reflection**

ᘓ **a time to look inside**

ᘓ **a time to trust**

ᘓ **a time to have faith**

ᘓ **a time to let go of everything around us**

a) The Importance Of The 'Mist'

We all need a bit of 'mist' in our lives and perhaps to use this time effectively and to reflect, to look back and see where we were yesterday and where we are today. What have we experienced so far? A feeling of being lost can open up the door to discover or look into the 'deeper' inner self, our own creative side, because there is nothing around us to look at and focus on, so this is when we ought to let go and concentrate on the inside.

The times for building a solid foundation, putting in structures and some rules are not important at this moment. There is no need to waste energy on this topic. The energy is focused to travel inside to get in touch with our inner playfulness and activate our creativity on a different level, which is quite important to take on board too. Some of us do forget that this part exists in all of us. These events from the outside, again a reminder of our cycles, are here to make sure that every part of us is activated and looked at, time by time, chapter by chapter. We can't play all our parts at once. They come when needed, ready to be shown, used and integrated on our journey.

Some unexplored parts can be uncomfortable, yes they can be. Everything is uncomfortable when seen and discovered for the first time. Feelings of hesitation and caution are presented. These particular times are here to enter into the shadows of our self or step down into the unknown, a bit like into the 'underworld' or the 'cellar'... this 'underworld/cellar' part can come with surprises, fears and a feeling of discomfort. What I mean is that we are ready and somehow deep inside we know it has to be done, our subconscious is calling big time! There is no rush, plenty of time to go to a place where vulnerability and pain will approach and face us. This is where the 'mist' comes in. There is no compass and no movement from the outside. That means the time has arrived to listen and observe, to let go and surrender. Some people fall asleep and go into destruction, numb themselves and blame whatever comes towards them. I am sure you can guess what I mean with destruction and numbness... it can be anything from drugs to alcohol but also a huge amount of food. Anything that will take you away from you and you can pretend. That is OK, for a while only! With this experience we learn how it feels like to go into these destructions and be numb – simply being asleep! Hopefully, you will move away from it and not repeat it too often. So, be aware, don't sleep away your whole life!

With little rituals, trust and belief, as I shared before, you can make sure that this sleep will be used for your benefit, to face what you have to face, to ask for help or guidance if needed, or even discover some new treasures. Naturally, we **are** thirsty and hungry for movement and for life... simply being fully present.

Again, some need longer and some need less time for their 'beauty sleep/being energised'. Our personality, our individuality, is different in each one of us. There is no comparison and competition. The way in which each of us approaches that situation is unique and special, remember! These 'misty' times are important in our lives for all of us. These events will lead and bring us closer to ourselves. Some funky ideas or even some great sparks can appear from nowhere. After a while the wind sets in again and we know how to use our sails to arrive at our destination, our next chapter, or even towards the beginning of a new dream. The determination is becoming really strong! Excitement kicks in. Our creativity is activated again. Perhaps a feeling or a memory from the past will touch us, connect to some beautiful memories, when being little, or/and in youth where excitement and creativity was unlimited will appear and touch us again.

b) The Holy Grail

Let me tell you in brief a story, a myth: the Arthurian Hero Parsifal's spiritual search for the quest – the Holy Grail – that fits beautifully in this paragraph.

There was a young man called Parsifal from a simple background who became a knight of King Arthur's Round Table because of his bravery, innocence and curiosity. Sometime in his early knighthood years, he found himself presented with the Holy Grail with a question towards him: 'Who shall I serve?' He wasn't aware of its meaning and the unique power behind it and refused to accept it. He walked away. Deep inside he knew and felt that he had left something very magical behind and came back a few years later to claim it. Unfortunately it was gone. He was searching for this Holy Grail all his life and could not find it. The meaning of the story is: the Holy Grail is our uniqueness, our purpose, the inner hero in us, our true authenticity that is always presented to us as a mirror in all kind of shapes, forms, people, events etc. We can't find the Holy Grail outside, it is not waiting or sitting somewhere for us to be found. It is in us, we are the Holy Grail. Only with awareness, a certain amount of life experience and a familiar pattern that repeats itself, meaning showing us to wake up and make changes so we can reach this Holy Grail.

The question: 'Who shall I serve?' The answer is: It is **me,** first I have to serve me with love, compassion, kindness etc. so I can serve my abundance, gift and knowledge to others.

c) An Exercise

Look back and see if there is a pattern that repeats itself, a pattern of excitement and creativity in certain stages in your life – just to put this thought out! Have a go if you are interested and discover when and how you expressed this uniqueness, this special feeling, your inner gift on your journey of life. Close your eyes and go through your life in your mind:

How old were you when you felt the excitement, your flow of your uniqueness?

In which form was the excitement?

How did it make you feel?

Where did it happen?

How long did it stay with you?

When did you experience this awesome feeling again?

How many years later?

How was it activated or who did activate this feeling of excitement for you?

Where were you at this time? In what stage of your life?

How long did it stay with you?

Write the answers in your journal and see where it leads you. Perhaps it could be used as an indicator. Where we feel excitement the energy of creativity flows very easily, almost no effort needed at all.

d) An Example

My life or myself, my subconscious approached a mist that was very uncomfortable and there was no sign of light wherever I looked. It forced me really to look at myself and my life around me. As I shared in Chapter 1, in my early adulthood experience, I started to paint, discovered self-development in different forms, reading and exploring Psychological Astrology. This kind of creativity and curiosity, my gift is in me... as we know, we all have our own unique gifts, please don't forget that! These gifts are not expressed all the time and are not visible all the time, unfortunately.

My gift was at home, in my own four walls, nicely expressed, in a very safe environment for a long time, for many years, without being pushed and challenged. This gift, the excitement, my flow of inner creativity, came and left a few times, in a period of quite a few years. Until I felt it was time to take it to another level, to take it outside of my comfort zone... meaning really outside, away from home and getting in touch with the outside world, other people than family and friends. My gut feeling, my instinct, led me naturally to start moving towards my destination. With a few steps in between of left and right, up and down – an inner dialogue of conversation and taking action... what I am saying is I was searching for something related to work on the internet. Out of the blue an interesting site popped up – three-year astrology course; my thought of studying astrology in London, becoming a student and travelling for higher education, formed a picture. I felt excitement, joy and a real sense of being in the right place at the right time.

Intuitive, I went to the opening day. It was a deep feeling of knowing that I had arrived at my destination. Everything was flowing without any disruption and boundaries. I finally enrolled and became a student. I was challenged big time! Reading material, preparation for coursework, writing assignments and presenting in the group. There was a lot of fear, yes a lot of it. However, my excitement was much bigger than my angst. My excitement pushed me through my limiting belief, pushed me to the edge of my comfort zone in all shapes and forms. Hence, my commitment was 100%, getting up early in the morning, 5.00 am, travelling four hours by train to attend my course. Then back, four hours travel, to get home and read, study and take my knowledge to the next level, not forgetting being a business owner, mother and wife.

I made time and I made it happen, a big no-no for excuses. The excitement was far too big and the timing was perfect – I was ready to pursue my dream. How it would manifest, I had no idea. We don't know, we can only assume and guess how our dreams might come alive. I can only say, I promise you it will be much bigger, more beautiful and vibrant, it will be even more exciting than you can ever imagine! Remember Chapter 5... we dream to be **the star,** don't forget we have to become the star first, having the confidence and strength so we can reach for the Holy Grail, our uniqueness, the gift that all of us carry inside.

No child can take the responsibility of leadership and guidance; growing up and some life experience is necessary to claim that kind of position. There is no way to accept wealth if we don't feel valued and accepted by ourselves the way we really are, no fakeness and illusion from the outside.

When you are really ready to become your 'Hero of Making'...

- ❧ **don't forget you are the captain**
- ❧ **don't forget there is no pressure**
- ❧ **don't forget to be asleep for too long**
- ❧ **don't forget that the opportunity for reaching out to your inner hero is in front of you**

> *You will be so surprised what the universe will give you and deliver in front of you.*
>
> *It is a bit like a beautiful colourful box wrapped with magic.*

We think we have an idea which is quite simple and basic. But actually, this idea is just a spark of what it will or might become. The time, it doesn't really matter. The time is here to form us to what we have to become and then prepare us for the sharing with others. By looking inside, finding and discovering our Holy Grail can be overwhelming from time to time. However, with the universal cycles, our inner growth will bring confidence, stability and wisdom that will lead to full expression of our gift. On our unique, bespoke journey we become:

- ❧ **the Creator, creating our own life**
- ❧ **the Artist, splashing some colours of joy and fun in different areas of our life, and hopefully regularly**

- the Designer, designing our own dream, having access to our unique gift, the purpose of fulfilling our destiny

- the Gardener, planting the seed of opportunities that was given to us and making sure of its healthy growth

- the Architect, building and maintaining a solid structure and foundation, even by being destroyed by others and Mother Nature, the cycles of our lives, and still having the wisdom and knowledge of expanding our true inner home

- the Parent, giving unconditional love, support and guidance for confidence, independence and individuality

- the Author, making sure everything is written down for our legacy for sharing and passing on to our future generations to come

- the Teacher, teaching gratitude, kindness and compassion

- the Leader, leading with passion, inspiration and truth, being a role model for everyone, the young and old, the poor and rich

e) Entrepreneurs Of The Future

We are the entrepreneurs of the future and the student for a lifetime. We have gained and we have some awareness – the awareness of yourself and knowing already how you 'tick'. That is a huge bonus and makes the steps for moving forward much easier. Knowing that it is a journey and whatever happens it is OK... of course when:

- ❧ **the heart is in the right place and**
- ❧ **spreads love and kindness and**
- ❧ **be and feel grateful and**
- ❧ **open to share the gift that you have inside you with others so their journey can become much smoother and really quite enjoyable**

However, whatever does excite us is in us already and needs/wants to be expressed with time. The time has its own meaning, a meaning of maturity, wisdom, awareness, solid foundation and stability in our personality and the beauty that wants to shine on all levels of our being. To say **I want it now** is a bit wasted – really wasted! It doesn't happen like that. Rome was not built in a day, nor are we. We need these times for ourselves, we need to experience certain levels of our beings – it is a vital growth for our fulfilment towards the dream and authenticity.

Back to my experience... With every study there is a lot of coursework, reading, seminars, attending weekend workshops, webinars... the importance of gaining the knowledge so that I am in a position of being able to help others. Painting is a different approach. Expression through colours creates a peaceful surrounding, takes me away from my routine, far away, and transports me into my magical space, where I can be, just be without any boundaries, I love it. It brings healing and connection within. Some of my paintings are hanging in beautiful homes and inspiring some amazing people, my heroes. I feel so grateful to be able to give and share my gift with the world. And this is the excitement, an excitement that takes me to ups and downs, left and right and sparkles everywhere. Welcome to the magic of the universe, the perfection in every way!

Big ideas can be scary and overwhelming and far reached.

So, just be aware how long you are asleep, if you can, of course. With awareness, kindness and acknowledgment it will support the time, your time of growth. Whatever it takes, be patient.

One moment of patience
May ward off great disaster;
One moment of impatience
May ruin a whole life.

- Chinese proverb -

You do choose where you want to be. The universal cycles are here:

ᗌ **to lead and guide you**

ᗌ **to put you asleep and also wake you up**

ᗌ **to plant the seed and let it grow**

ᗌ **to destroy and to build your foundations again and again... this is part of all of us, our inner and outer journey – let's make it count, together!**

Your family, your friends and even the whole world can believe in you and still none of it really matters if you don't believe in you, in your beautiful self –

*it is all in your hands, you choose...
be awake and aware.*

View at *www.jasminkahansson.com*

CHAPTER NINE

The Truth Is Actually Of Letting Go So You Can Grow Up

WE ARE all holding on to a lot of things: holding on to memories, holding on to the past or even reliving in our minds the past from day to day. It is a bit like escaping into the foggy dream world and staying there almost forever... remember in the last chapter talking about being asleep?! One year is passing, another year is passing and then all of a sudden many years are gone and nothing was and is changed. The motivation is gone too and it is easier to stay where we are now, being asleep! Change becomes too difficult and to change a habit is a tricky one! It is too much effort to make a move; too many steps have to be taken to climb the mountain to be able to see another view, to breathe fresh air and feel the independence... hmmm! The word 'action' doesn't exist in our vocabulary anymore. I am sure it does in our foggy dream – 'the escaping and pretending mechanism'.

So, it is much easier to stay where we are now, in our 'day in and day out', the survival mechanism being and staying in the foggy dream world. Where we fall asleep and like to stay asleep, as I shared in the previous chapter. If the sleep goes too long, the energy, our inner flow gets stuck i.e. at home, in the relationship/ partnership, family, friendships, workplace, health etc. Heaviness comes into our sphere; a feeling of tiredness and frustration kicks in. These energies will create a habit around us that will reflect ourselves inside and outside. If you remember the mirror – it will show a posture of heavy shoulders, head down etc. If we do the same we will get the same.

Blaming and pointing a finger at the outside will come quite naturally. Consider and/or get familiar with a different approach, perhaps to look in your mirror, clean the dusty mirror and look at yourself, truly look at you and play with the idea of…

ଔ **letting go and moving on**

ଔ **making changes or stepping out of**
   your comfort zone

ଔ **hmmm… is it scary or even can it be fulfilling?**

Of course, changes or getting out of a difficult state won't happen in a second. The first step is the awareness and clarity, to take responsibility for these 'sleeping' actions and face it with honesty:

ଔ **yes, I am sleeping**

ଔ **yes, I don't want to look at the mirror**

ଔ **yes, I don't want to make changes in myself etc.**

As we all know, the list can be quite long of the state where we are at. However, the word responsibility is a growing-up word. With responsibility comes commitment, which leads to structure and develops to strength. By just realising the state where we are and acknowledging it, it will start to shift, even a little bit. The state of the mind is starting to move towards excitement, something positive is happening. A bit like the window is a tiny bit open for fresh air. Let's open the window more and let properly fresh air in and start to breathe and perhaps to look at the sun for a moment. It is scary to wake up and then have to realise what really happened.

Yes, the time is here to let go fully and embrace what is in front. It is time to grow up, time to let go of the past. Exciting times are ahead. Your spirit, your essence is ready to take the next step and is urging you to move forward. The old stuff, the past, has to be left behind or at least some of it. The time is here to create new things which are light and easy to carry.

> 'The past is history, the future is mystery
> and the present is a GIFT.'
>
> - Lisa Unger -

a) Daughter And Mother Story

A friend's story, a story about a daughter and mother relationship/dynamic.

The daughter was a very successful business owner, had a great company and was good at her job for many years. Somehow, the excitement started to fade; she still felt OK and was quite 'happy' in the business. Time went and she went with it too. A year was gone, another year went and all of a sudden many years passed. Somehow she felt that she had to change something and took the step of responsibility. Her mother, on the other side, was not happy with her change. It was her mother's wish to continue the business and bring more success home. The mother wanted her dream to be lived through her daughter. The daughter felt guilty and frustrated for many years; she didn't want to disappoint her mother and followed her wish regardless.

The easiest way is to be asleep and stay asleep. It is much more difficult to face her mother and the situation that she is in. Management and leading a business wasn't difficult for the daughter so she stayed where she started many years ago and accepted it. Finally, the little window was opened and let a bit of breeze in.

I talked in the first chapter about the cycles, the universal cycles. These cycles activate, push, destroy... bring challenges and turn them into opportunities, when we allow it. The daughter started to realise that actually it was time to take responsibility, break the invisible link between her mother and her. Of course it is not easy to face a situation that is quite solid and grounded with family belief and patterns. However, she decided, a strong urge from the inside, to cut off the invisible link, the old pattern, the past and leave mother's dream behind and find her true colour.

Is it scary or fulfilling? Actually it is both. A brave action with a lot of courage leads to fear and discomfort, but also at the same time it is a fulfilling feeling of achievement, being responsible for that step in your own way, a feeling of being grown up and becoming your own adult.

With this action of letting go, she attracted other signs, completely different signs, signs from the outside. She had always had the dream to buy land and build her own farm. As a little girl she loved to be outside, connecting with nature and having/living a simple life. And guess what, she pursued her dream and is very happy where she is today. Her mother is another story.

b) Movements Are Vital

We have to leave the old stuff behind and make space for new things. The old stuff is heavy to carry and it is outgrown anyway. Movements are vital and bring us back to basics. With movements we shift energy, we shift the state of the mind and the body. Even little movements will bring change from the inside and outside. When we start to shift inside, little things will start to change from the outside... just remember the mirror chapter.

Let's imagine... let's say that we think we can't change, as sometimes a little voice tells us here and there, regularly, all the time! Hmmm, I am sure you know what I mean. So, we can start from the outside at our home.

Look at your home:

- ❧ **What does your kitchen look like?**
- ❧ **What does your bedroom look like?**
- ❧ **What does your bathroom look like?**
- ❧ **What does your dining area look like?**
- ❧ **What docs your utility room look like?**
- ❧ **What does your toilet look like?**

Have a good look and see what is around you. Do you like it or not?

- ❧ **How messy is it?**
- ❧ **How much old stuff is lying around?**
- ❧ **How much paper is covering the worktops?**
- ❧ **How much floor space is covered with stuff?**
- ❧ **Are your plants or flowers alive, dusty or dried out?**
- ❧ **How heavy is your handbag that you carry daily?**
- ❧ **How old is your makeup?**
- ❧ **How many products are lying around in the bathroom?**

The list can be quite looooooong but I stop here. I am sure you get the idea. With decluttering the house you will invite new energy. At the same time you 'clean up' your mind and let in fresh and new ideas, finally letting go of the old ones and being in charge of it too. Also at the same time the word responsibility pops in. You are doing something great, making space for new things – excellent and well done **you**! By being active in this way you will open up to your own creativity naturally. Something will happen from the outside, you are starting to attract new mirrors... new people, events in all kind of shapes and forms. The process of letting go is giving you the opportunity for growing up and starting something different, something new. With this great achievement in yourself you will feel fulfilled, have fresh energy and be ready to take on the next challenge and turn it into **your** great opportunity.

Don't forget to celebrate every achievement with style, recognition and gratefulness. Every step, every climb, every change, every realisation and every mirror that is presented to you – it is an achievement, **a big achievement,** meaning you are moving forward and getting closer to who you really are.

Growing up is something beautiful, where strength, wisdom and knowledge always play a big part.

Growing up brings independence and freedom.

Growing up brings leadership and guidance.

Growing up brings your inner teacher out.

Growing up is maturity in all forms and shapes.

Growing up brings style and class
– Audrey Hepburn pops into my mind!

Growing up is something where you can start to share your experiences with the world and help others to become who they want to become one day...

... and this is really exciting...

*being part of a movement of changing
and helping others!*

With our amazing, individual, unique gift that we all
have in ourselves, it comes out when we are ready, ready
to shine and have the confidence in ourselves. Each
gift, each one of us, that starts to share this uniqueness
with others, help others on their journey, we become
their mirrors. And imagine that everyone brings this
energy to Mother Earth, our true home, step by step,
person by person, family by family, home by home,
community by community, town by town, county by
county, country by country – it is endless...

- THIS IS WHAT I CALL MAGIC -

*PS: just be aware, it is a journey and it will take time...
a little reminder to make sure to get grounded and
stay grounded, if possible, as long as possible; and let's
start, let's start to bring your creativity out, step by step.
However, you have to start somewhere! Just one step, it
takes only one step to shake up the energy that leads to
the excitement of waking up your creativity for accessing
your inner gift that is waiting to be seen and shared with
all of us!*

CHAPTER TEN

The Time Will Take Off Your Fake Masks

LIFE IS a bit like playing on the stage, playing different parts in our life, different parts of our self at certain times. When we are born, we 'arrive' on Mother Earth with our own individual blueprint, our DNA, our destiny, and our purpose. We are arriving completely pure and innocent. With time, years to come, we start to put layers on and create masks depending on our parents/caretaker and the environment. With growing up and being in different stages of our development we learn very quickly how we need to behave or act to get certain things for feeling loved and accepted. When we are tiny, at the beginning of our new life, it is the crying for attention, comfort and love, screaming for food, milk and nappy changing. Crying for attention and being heard and seen is actually the main survival instinct. Cuddles and being held is one of the important contacts at the first stage of life.

We learn very soon how we need to behave to get what we need and want. When we look at little ones and observe them, we can see in their behaviour what they want, by being sweet, cuddly, smiley or even with their tantrums, anger and frustration. It depends on the parents or the caretaker how they approach the situation or the challenge; this is when the masks start to take shape and form. Masks are built for a reason to survive the situations we are in. The masks are mainly for protection and to become what the surrounding, our society, wants from us. Under the mask is still our true self, hidden from the outside. Our essence will come out when we are ready to unleash our true unique self and take responsibility for who we really are. This is when the masks will come off.

a) The Importance Of The Masks

On our journey, our life journey, we need these masks:

ೲ **for receiving love, but also**

ೲ **for being loved**

ೲ **for giving love and**

ೲ **for pretending by being someone else**

Somehow it is quite important to experience all these different masks that we inherited from our family and even from our generation; to see how it feels playing these parts in our life. Of course what we show outside is not really what we are inside. From the outside we present ourselves the way that is needed to be seen, demanded or accepted... we get used to it, having these masks on all the time. However, time will give us the opportunity to learn from them and with time finally we will be able to take the masks off. Trust me, keeping the masks will not be a lifetime, it will be just for a certain period of time. I mean, a certain period of time until the energy from above, if you remember the life cycles, the universal cycles, start to deliver a certain situation that will challenge you – the time for change is approaching! With this challenge you are able to start to realise:

- Actually the mask makes me feel uncomfortable
- I have outgrown it
- It doesn't fit me anymore
- I don't like this 'fake smile'
- Yes, I can do this without pretending to be someone else
- I want to find out more about who and what is behind this mask
- I am ready to show me, little by little, step by step

These masks became a part of you, you are not even aware that you have one on. When you think, yes, that is me... well, these masks are not really you. They are just here to protect you from the outside, mainly from people:

- who are judging you
- who are blaming you for all kind of reasons
- who are trying to destroy your dreams

- who are feeding from your energy
- who are jealous of your achievements
- who are pretending to be part of you

We have these masks on at home, at work, with our friends and we know exactly which one to put on depending on the environment and the people around us. We do it so naturally and unaware that it is not a big deal, really. We don't know anything else. Why would we think that we have a mask on? The mask has become a part of our self, a big part of our life. Again, don't forget that these masks are our protection to feel safe and be safe. People see us in a certain way and we are quite happy to show them ourselves in a certain way.

> *We don't see things as they are,*
> *we see things as we are.*

Well, with certain times, with the certain steps on your path...

- when you become aware, positively aware
- when you have a real consciousness about your true self
- when you have discovered your unique gift and when you know how you tick, where the excitement starts to explode inside
- when the sails are set towards your destination
- when you don't care anymore what the outside is thinking about you

⚮ when your mirror is nicely dusted, cleaned
and polished

⚮ when your rituals are part of your routine,
almost daily

... these masks will slowly disappear from you and your life. Feeling gratitude for serving you on your journey, for helping and protecting you in difficult situations. Remember, these masks were created by your life and were fulfilling their tasks to protect you from the outside and they have been part of the shaping of your destiny... hmmm, what is left then? Yes, **you** – the pure and amazing 'I'...

I **am** special

I **am** unique

I **am** me!

CHAPTER ELEVEN

Only You Have The Key

WE ALL want to be the best, do the best, and strive for the best possible that we can achieve. The search becomes endless and can get quite tiring.

But actually the best is in us already, we are the BEST!

Whatever it is it will come out eventually, yep it will! Looking for the 'best', it seems like we all somehow always search on the outside and even try to copy others. Thinking, yes, this looks great, the person is fantastic, amazing, awesome. However, it is good to have role models, to be inspired and motivated. As you remember in Chapter 6, we are all a mirror for each other. What we admire in others is in us too. It has to be discovered first that this quality is already inside.

So, back to the key... this is where the key comes in, our unique special key. Only you have the key, only you can use your key to open the door to your unique individual potential. No one else! The key is with you all the time. Unfortunately, it is forgotten by being busy with life and dealing with 101 things at the same time. The key is still sitting somewhere safe, out of reach and not seen anymore... forgotten! The search is continuing... still searching endlessly to find this **best** that we aim to fulfil.

Actually, when we really think, how does this **best** express itself? Hmmm, imagine there is no pressure of being perfect – nice isn't it?! Unfortunately, the outside is bombarding and pressuring us regularly with the media, which leads us, of course, to the endless search of perfection that doesn't really exist! No one is perfect otherwise we would not be human. So, without this 'dreamed up' pressure... just being still for a moment, finding a little time to be still for a few minutes, in here and now...

Imagine you have a glass wall built all around you and nothing from the outside is affecting you. Every unwelcome energy that is bombarding you is bouncing back, far away from you. Being protected from the outside the moment of freedom will expand and lead to a blissful:

- ❧ **natural feeling of being able to centre yourself and stay relaxed for a moment**
- ❧ **natural feeling of being comfortable in your own skin**
- ❧ **natural flow of harmony**
- ❧ **natural flow of your own energy**

We tap into our creativity, a taste of excitement, joy, happiness – you name it, it follows; the creativity opens our flow of this amazing, unique, special, awesome, magical energy!

a) The Word Creativity

Perhaps you might ask 'what is creativity?' or say 'I am not creative'. Just for your information what the definition for the word creativity in general means:

The use of imagination or original ideas to create something; inventiveness; divine inspiration; creativity is a phenomenon whereby something new and somehow valuable is formed; the created item may be intangible such as an idea, a scientific theory, a musical composition or a joke, or a physical object such as an invention, a literary work or a painting.

adj. inventive, imaginative, original, artistic, inspired, visionary, talented, gifted, resourceful, ingenious, clever, productive, fertile.

○ **We all are creators**

○ **We all have the ability to make something from nothing**

○ **We all have unique and individual ideas**

○ **We all have access to our inner source of endless abundance**

When we have the time, or even **make time,** just a little bit of time, which will bring us in the natural feeling of being blissful, centred and relaxed, I am 100% certain that we will tap into this beautiful flow of creativity in us.

Today, with the time running like crazy, a lot of pressure from the outside to achieve something that really doesn't belong to us, not our purpose, which is showing us on a regular basis on TV, in magazines, on social media etc. how to be what they tell us to be. Actually, that is not how we can tap into our source of uniqueness. However, when we experience pain or a situation of discomfort, something does happen (remember that being aware is your own guidance for a better understanding of yourself) and we can have access to this amazing flow of abundance in us.

It can be something very simple like... may I share a story with you?

> *As you know, I am a mother. When my children were little, they needed a lot of stimulation, guidance and of course to have fun too. As with every parent, I want the best for my children. Being the best is exhausting and we put a lot of pressure on ourselves to be the best parent. Following a guideline by someone else, a guideline that is put in front of us by the media that is around us all the time. We are not perfect, we are still humans and not angels.*

There were times where I felt burnt out, tired, short-tempered and unable to give my whole attention to the little ones. Not being 100% present in here and now, the kids knew how to press my buttons. Not because they are mean or to upset Mummy. What they needed was very different from what I needed at that moment. So, I asked myself the question: What can I do to change this uncomfortable situation that makes me irritated and is leading to frustration and anger? I didn't give room for a 'why me?' question, a feeling of being the victim, that would lead to feeling useless and not a good mother... all this negativity that would bring me low frequencies and really feel 'useless'. As you remember, words have power. It is our choice choosing the negative side or the positive side.

So, I stopped at that right moment, where I felt enough is enough! I focused for a moment on my breathing to collect my anger and frustration. Guess what? In this very moment of breathing and focusing I tapped into my creativity. For my way of dealing with my little ones I used my inner creativity in a playful way. Let's dress up, I thought, and let's build a stage.

The first step was to put the music on. Intuitively I have chosen shamanism music, Indian energy, drums etc. Leading and guiding the kids to this fantastic expression of play, we all got very excited. In our house we have a room where we do all this 'crazy' stuff. My creativity comes alive and also theirs *is in action. The children have the opportunity to tap into their unique expression of themselves.*

I created a play in front of them and let them choose the way they wanted to express themselves. The creativity started to flow and flourish beautifully. We have a box full of dressing-up clothes, fabrics and actually a lot of stuff that can be used for anything. Seeing the kids being so excited, their little eyes lit up, full of sparkles – that gave me more energy to be present. With the music, makeup and dressing-up clothes we started to use the drums and made a really proper noise. We danced in a circle and screamed out as much as we could. The release of anger and frustration had been transformed into a playful and colourful energy.

Three things were expressed in this situation:

❧ First was – frustration and anger was transformed into something beautiful; a release of the inner emotion was able to come out in a positive way

❧ Second was – through discomfort or pain I was able to connect with my creativity and use it in a positive way

❧ The third was – I was the parent that the kids needed: I gave them structure, a safe environment for their expression and I became the leader and teacher for them

I believe that dancing, jumping or any kind of activity combined with music and sound will loosen up tension that is created naturally by doing 101 things at once, mentally, emotionally or physically. By moving the body without any structure and restriction, the will of freedom and 'craziness' will activate the natural flow of inner release. It ticks a few boxes:

- releasing the inner tension
- activating the creativity
- transforming the frustration into playfulness
- filling the lungs with air/breathing again
- being in here and now
- bringing grounding
- far away from 101 things
- connecting with the natural flow and
- having fun... smiling or even laughing

b) The Inner Wound

I know when we are able to express our frustration and anger in a positive creative movement a lot of healing can be achieved. Yes, the mind, being in a positive and creative mode, using the right words, focusing and looking at the bright side, it is important. But if we can't get the emotions out then I believe it starts to bubble up inside. Bubbling up too many times, closing up and being in uncomfortable moments for too long will open up the 'wound' that we like to ignore, or is put aside nicely, or even we are not aware of it at all.

Yes, it is true, we all carry a 'wound' inside that started somewhere from the beginning of our first stage of life. It can be anything from birth, childhood, parent or parents to relationships, loss, children, work, self-belief/value, finances etc. I am sure we all have that kind of list somewhere in us. This wound is somewhere deep inside and it doesn't show the 'bleeding'. It expresses in ways that it starts to be uncomfortable and of course with time painful. That brings us... it sounds perhaps crazy... but this wound keeps us alive. When we feel this wound, the discomfort is where we have the opportunity to tap into our creativity. Our essence leads us to this place and asks subconsciously for awareness and recognition. It wants and needs healing. It wants and needs to be looked at. As we are all individual, special and unique we will express our wounds in different ways and also our creativity.

A myth story: **the wounded healer**

In Greek mythology the wounded healer was Chiron, the god of healing and immortal. His lower body was half horse and upper body half human. As a baby he was rejected and abandoned by his parents. God Apollo took him under his wings and taught him music, poetry, and art in every form. Later in his life he became a mentor and teacher to the king's sons and Greek heroes. Unfortunately Chiron was wounded by his student Hercules with a poison arrow that he had taught Hercules to make.

Even being the god of healing, he could not heal himself. He lived with incredible pain until he chose to give up his immortality for Prometheus who stole fire from the gods and brought it to mankind.

The wounded healer, its healing journey, teaches to develop a consciousness both rational and intuitive; coming home to itself, connected to heaven and earth and allowing the energy to flow between them.

Much of your pain is self-chosen.

It is the bitter potion by which the physician within you heals your sick self.

Therefore trust the physician, and drink his remedy in silence and tranquility:

For his hand, though heavy and hard, is guided by the tender hand of the Unseen.

- Kahlil Gibran -

In life we will clean the wound many times and try to find the needle (remember Chapter 1, shaping and forming our tools) to stitch it. The wound will open up until we find the right needle, the right thread so we can stitch it with patience, and the knowledge how to stitch it properly so it doesn't bleed anymore.

By healing this inner wound we become our own inner healer. When the wound is healed we become the healer for others. With our experience, our collected knowledge on our path and our grown wisdom we are able to help and support others and share our own shaped tool. Of course, it will not happen in a moment, today or tomorrow. It is a time thing, a process that will bring the healing. At the beginning we think it is not a big deal, we can cope with it. We are busy creating a life, building a relationship, collecting our knowledge and so on. There is not much or not enough time to spare and also not much wisdom and life experience. These experiences that we encounter through our life, on our path, these experiences will:

- shape our personality
- make us strong
- make us confident
- make us certain
- make us grow
- give us wisdom
- give us acceptance for who we are
- bring us self-love
- bring us self-worth
- take the layers off our protections
- wake up our own teacher and healer

c) We Will Shine

There comes a point where we don't care anymore what the outside is thinking of us. Feeling and being centred in ourselves will shine so much love and harmony that the caring energy will flow to inspire and activate others. We learn from our own criticism, doubts and ego but on the other hand we learn also from compassion, love and support.

Our mind is the driver and will provide us the map where:

ᘒ **we have to go**

ᘒ **we will go**

ᘒ **and we want to go**

The body, our temple, also something that we choose consciously or unconsciously.

Either:

ᘒ **it can be our temple to be cared for with love, kindness and we nurture it with the right ingredients; I believe the right ingredients are if you listen very carefully, your body will tell you exactly what it needs**

ᘒ **or we destroy it, not wanting it to be seen as a part of our self, it is treated as a separation from the soul!**

I believe we have to experience both ways to understand which one will lead to positive results. This process will give us the knowledge and the awareness of what the body really requires, the fuel for keeping and staying healthy. Having a healthy body and caring for it like a temple really does bring a feeling of great fulfilment. All these steps, the process, will start to make us consciously aware of our inner wound and requires a closer look to find a way of healing. As I mention repeatedly, we are all unique and different. There is no right or wrong. We will approach it the way we feel is perfect for us.

I will explain in more detail through my story. When I was little I had difficulties with speech. I was unable to speak in front of people. When the teacher pointed me out to read a paragraph or learn a poem and share it in the classroom with all the students, I disappeared into the ground, it became very difficult and uncomfortable. Me, standing up and trying to share, I could not say a word. There was a blockage inside me that could not be taken away. I stood there moving my lips but nothing came out, no sound, no word. That knocked my confidence completely and led to no friends. No one was interested in spending time with me.

I learned early on to survive by escaping in my dream world. I got on with school life, did my homework etc. Many years passed and life as it is, of course, caught up with me with more stuff. The pain became bigger and I was unable to deal with it. So, I asked for help inside and help came from the outside.

A book about astrology crossed my path. The understanding of energy and stars led to the next level of help. I started actively to work on myself with psychosynthesis, which then led to family constellation. Through these therapies, allowing me to go deeper in myself, looking into the blockage, taking some layers off my protection, it opened up my inner artist, as I mentioned at the beginning of the book. The pain, my discomfort, my blockage pushed me to take action. The action towards body movement, at that time shamanism music, manifested itself in taking the brushes and going really crazy. I expressed the anger almost in a 'tantrum' way and used colours that I connected to pain. My first painting was actually the release of my holding back emotions/frustration and became an amazing healing process.

The healing, my inner healing, started to take place and I also realised that I have the key, my creativity to my inner potential, my purpose. By using this key I was able to access this amazing **me** and finally started to let go and grow.

Whatever this expression is and whichever way it is expressed, that is your own blueprint, your own unique DNA. That is your special gift. My expression was and still is in colours and stars.

The journey, our life journey, will make this unique gift that we all have recognised, bring it alive, and it will reflect in events and people. The mirrors will appear and show us what we are presenting. How beautiful is that!

Yesterday you were a child with playfulness and curiosity – unconscious of today... Today you are using your own key to your beautiful self – with consciousness... and tomorrow you become the leader for others by sharing your wisdom, your experience and your uniqueness – it becomes your legacy.

By being your own healer, you heal your own wounds, which will open up your creativity. With time we are learning more about ourselves and collecting knowledge through books, seminars, workshops, adventure, exploring the world, meeting people, experiencing relationships, involvement in communities, helping others etc. This gift will be coming out, step by step, to be shaped and formed the way that you are designed, with your unique personality. This natural flow will be touching and inspiring many of us.

So, whatever experience is needed to find out and to discover that you have your own key, either forgotten or put away somewhere safe...

... look for it, reach for it and be grateful for the guidance that is leading you to this beautiful and unique 'I'.

View at *www.jasminkahansson.com*

CHAPTER TWELVE

Everything Is OK

EVERY DECISION we make will and does lead to our unique, specially created and designed destiny. A destiny that is imprinted in our own blueprint, DNA, our personality and very own makeup. Whatever decision is made it is important for the next move. Changes in all forms, from little to big, included with all emotions, from pain to love, are vital and part of our journey. Learning about our own gut feeling, learning to be understood about how we really tick and how it feels to be authentic and follow the instinct that arises on a regular basis on this unique path. We all have our own Hero that wants and needs to shine. The path that we call life will bring us the necessary lessons and tools for our Hero to learn confidence, strength, warmth and kindness. The times will be scary but also exciting.

We will kill the big dragon and climb the big mountain to save the 'princess' that is us:

- ❦ We will walk on rose petals and also walk on fire
- ❦ We will cross rivers and also get stuck in mud
- ❦ We will feel exhaustion and also lose our energy on destructions
- ❦ We will have a broken heart only to learn how to heal it
- ❦ We will experience loss and experience the infinity of love
- ❦ We will attract chaos but also peace
- ❦ We will experience inner freedom for knowing everything is possible
- ❦ We will build structure and security for forming our stability
- ❦ We will destroy our foundation and start building again
- ❦ We will build our own muscle to be able to fight back and protect ourselves from others, the outside

All these challenges and all the beauty that is around us all the time is just LIFE.

- ❦ Whatever you do it is OK
- ❦ Whatever you attract it is OK
- ❦ Whatever you decide it is OK
- ❦ Whatever you move it is OK

There are really no rules, no instructions or a manual/handbook, only the universal rules, the cosmic order provides you with everything that is needed for your own growth to become who you really and truly are. Unfortunately it comes with pain, discomfort and frustration that are 'nicely' delivered from the outside. Always for your benefit! These experiences, as I mentioned, belong to this amazing journey. Being the Hero is not something that comes easily, of course not. There will be the time where the Hero will shine with its whole and own glory and lead others, for their future, to the same or similar path of experiences:

- from unconscious to conscious
- from unawareness to awareness
- from fear to love
- from pain to transformation
- from blaming to forgiveness
- from taking to giving and sharing
- from blaming to taking responsibility
- from being the victim to become the true and real leader
- from I to we

a) There Is No Rush

To become this amazing beautiful 'I' that you have already in you is just waiting to be transformed. So, please remember there is no rush, no hurry and no competition. The universal cycles will make sure that you are awake and fully present. I believe we all have this knowledge and if we all know that, whatever we do is OK. Perhaps the world would be more awake, relaxed and focused and would see the journey as part of self-discovery. If we have the kindness to honour and respect what comes towards us, the energy around us will change immediately and bring an inner harmony, comfort and peace.

Respect and honour are quite big words and full of amazing vibration that comes in all colours and brings something magical. Mind, body and spirit to be respected and honoured – can you imagine how the beauty will surround you? Imagine you use the word temple, on a regular basis, for the body and really give it the right fuel, meaning what the body needs and requires, and not you. Don't forget that your Hero is destined to kill the dragon, climb the mountain and save the princess – **you!** With a healthy body and strong mind, it would of course be much easier and straightforward. I am just putting it out again as I talked about it before.

b) A Little Exercise

An exercise that I know will give you a nice guidance, more understanding of yourself, your amazing awesome Hero.

Take a moment out of your daily routine and find a room, a spot where you can be with your beautiful self.

Put on a nice piece of music that will spellbind you in your magical world, your own special place, which you can create every time when you enter this magical place. Again, just a reminder, go with your flow, there are no rules. You are your own creator. If sometimes the magical world doesn't appear, please don't worry. The feeling of peace without pictures... it is OK too (I love classical music, it brings a peaceful vibration i.e. Mozart).

I am sure you have your special notebook with you, perhaps by now all the time. List three weaknesses and three strengths, in two columns – keep it as simple as possible. Be honest and bold. Spend some time with these words and feel them – each one of them. How does it make you feel? Now you can paint them, draw them or just write your feelings, express it in a way that resonates with you.

Now imagine these words shake hands with each other. One by one, one word with another word. Observe your body, really observe and feel it... what does the body do when you put them together? How is your breathing doing? How is your posture doing? How are your shoulders doing? Just recognise it and stay with it, with your awareness. Be with these emotions and feel them, breathe in and breathe out. By breathing in you make your tummy like a balloon, by breathing out you empty it and the tummy becomes very flat; go with the flow. Let go of everything that is in your mind and around you. No cheating! It is very important that you stay with this feeling.

With this flow of honesty and respect you are creating a bond between these words. Again, feel the bond and breathe in and breathe out, tummy big and tummy flat. Go with the flow. Whatever position you are with your body, put your head up and focus up in the air (I like to think the stars are around me and twinkling the energy from above). Again, what comes naturally to you, go with your own flow. Imagine saying the words respect and honour, either with your voice or inside. Stay with it and feel it.

Feel each one…

I respect myself

I honour myself

I respect myself

I honour myself

I respect myself

I honour myself

Your heart will expand and be filled with magical sparkles. Your magical sparkles that might or even will explode inside and spread out in your whole body… a bit like a thunderstorm (in my experience – again what you feel is perfect for your uniqueness). Feel it and stay with it, breathe in and breathe out, **breathe in and breathe out – these are your own sparkles,** the connection with the cosmic energy. Your weaknesses and your strengths are part of you and by connecting them together you already build a strong muscle to do what you have to do with your own magical 'I'... how beautiful and amazing is this – remember...

I **am** special
I **am** unique
I **am** me!

CHAPTER THIRTEEN

Use Your Own Magic Box

WE ALL have our own magic box. A very special box full of goodies, unique and magical to us. A box full of life experience, a fantastic collection of great life tools from early age until today, to be used and shared with everyone around us, our family, our friends and the community. With time, life experience and wisdom these tools turn into magic. These magical tools have beautiful power and can sparkle really bright and strong. The beauty that shines through is our confidence, our security in ourselves with a big smile of happiness. Don't forget that only you can put these sparkles out and only you know how to use these magical tools.

Why do I call them magical tools in the magic box? Because we all, each one of us, have our own unique journey, our own unique experience on Mother Earth with its 101 challenges ready and prepared for our own growth. So, how do we become who we are, every one of us – hmmm… do we need to do certain things in our life to 'hear' our inner call? On this path of challenges we start to collect help in different shapes and forms.

I would like to share a story with you, related to business. Being a business owner, the business comes with interesting challenges and great opportunities. Before we see these challenges transformed into opportunities, it is a 'little' gap between these two words!

The staff challenged the business of my husband and me, for a long period of time. Neither I nor my husband knew how to approach the situation, the tension between them and us started to become really uncomfortable. In our minds we thought we were doing the right thing: being kind, very helpful and always supportive and considerate for their own demands.

However, we were not the leaders or the business owners that they needed, and of course demanded. With time the staff started to bring and create chaos and in the end they all left. I was devastated and blamed them for my emotions. The outside created the victim in myself but actually I behaved that way and attracted a situation to experience that kind of feeling, which also led to opening my eyes and asking and pushing for change. It took me a while to realise that it was actually my doing. I had to change something. I had to approach the situation from a completely different view.

I stayed for a while in this chaos of emotions and felt very sorry, really sorry for myself. I could not believe how this could happen (as we all do when a situation approaches us and brings changes that we don't like but know it was time to do something completely different). My mum travelled from Vienna, came to help with the kids and finally I started to take the lead in our business, but only step by step. I was very nervous, insecure in myself, and I did not like at all what I had to do. With this uncomfortable feeling I needed to shift my mind into action. I read '101' books, attended '101' webinars and '101' seminars. Yes, I put my actions into 'Speedy Gonzales' gear. My focus spread some light on my achievements. A feel-good factor arose and gave me confidence in my steps. I started to love the changes inside and outside. Step by step I moved where I needed to be or wished to see myself. My mind and my actions helped me to achieve the position of the business where it wanted to be.

With this confidence I attracted interesting people and events. We met an amazing couple and they became our mentor and coach. They gave us tools for the business, so we could finally become the business owners and leaders for our team. It did not happen overnight, of course, it took some years to form and shape these tools called 'business', everything around the business, the inside and outside.

It was not easy, however it was interesting to observe and follow the energy of how things from the outside deliver the perfect energy to work with and grow with it.

Great attitude, not giving in, being and staying focused, and welcoming new challenges that with time turn into opportunities. The situation that we, my husband and I, created for ourselves – with this sadness, or sudden change, chaos and feeling like the victims – actually, it brought us beautiful opportunities, amazing tools, great confidence and strength for our next chapters.

Today I love to share my experiences and also these tools with people who are willing and prepared to take it on, learn from it and use them for themselves on their journey. My tools, shared and given to you, will become unique when you put your own sparkles on it, mixed with your personality, your own makeup. No tool is the same. We are all different individuals with our own special uniqueness. It makes me feel very happy and grateful to be able to help and support others in similar situations.

Everyone will benefit from your experience, from your own unique collection. You can share your magic box and help others enormously.

'Let's build together a long table and share.'

Sometimes, or even quite often, depending on our emotional wellbeing, we do forget our tools and like to be in the 'victim' stage. We leave the box in the corner and don't think about it anymore. We might be mainly focusing on problems and like to blame others. At this time it might feel easier to go through a 'poor me' challenge. Sometimes life takes over and we forget that we need to look closer at what is happening around us, like my story that I shared with you just a moment ago. It would be great to remember, when you can and want, of course, that the tools are here already, with you, and can be used any time when needed or when you are ready.

And also, our creation likes to hide sometimes and doesn't like to feel or be seen as special and unique. Actually, the feeling 'poor me' takes over and likes to sulk. Hmmm, we all like to sulk, don't we? Here and there, a short moment and/or a long period of time...

So, let's focus and concentrate on what is here now:

- Let's see where the energy flows easily, without any boundaries
- Let's see what comes easily, without any struggles or discomfort
- Let's see what you are good at (usually we like to deny it!)
- Let's see what your friends are saying about you
- Let's see how your friends would describe you

Ask your family members, your friends and your work colleagues about you. How would they describe you?

- What keywords would they use for you?
- What animal would suit your picture?
- What colour would be used to paint you?

It really doesn't matter what people think about you or what comments they have about you. It is a great exercise for receiving some interesting feedback from the outside, to see and realise how amazing and awesome you are. Be grateful for comments and compliments.

You might be surprised or you might even think, yes I know! Focus and concentrate on that beautiful person called 'I' – what is here already and turn it over and approach it differently.

It is quite simple, too simple actually... that simple... a bit like when we smile people smile back. Our hearts warm up and we look and feel happier. The world around us turns into a colourful picture.

a) A Smile And Much More

I do remember one interesting challenge that still puts a smile on my face after a number of years. When my kids were little and we needed to do the daily routine, a routine that took us out of the house, away from the comfort and safety. One of the weekly routines was the shopping, shopping with little ones – OMG! I am sure every parent knows what I mean. Of course, to start with I did the shopping online, home delivery etc. But somehow it was time to introduce the kids to a routine and invite them to experience something very different.

So, I thought, how can I make the experience, the trip to the supermarket, enjoyable and fun for all of us? A huge challenge, and it was and stayed a huge challenge...

for a while. Until I had enough, and started to change my mind, shifted my energy bundle, making space for new thoughts, my creative side that I left hidden somewhere in the corner, forgotten that it exists. Guess what, as I mentioned before, when you open up your uniqueness, your amazing 'I', the energy flows, it flows when no thinking is involved. The energy flows freely because it comes quite easily – this is what you are good at, your unique gift that we all have somewhere out there either forgotten, hidden or we are not even conscious of it.

OK, back to my story... so before we went on this trip to the supermarket, I sat down with the kids at the table and informed them what we were going to do: shopping time for cooking for our nice meal.

First we decided what we were going to have on our menu, second we needed to write all the things on the list. The kids realised they needed a list, a so-called shopping list, and a pen to make sure that we had it written down, not to be forgotten. Just to remind you, the kids were two and three years old at that time, no writing skills and not much letter knowledge. I had my paper and my pen in front of me and they also had their paper and their pen in front of them. We wrote down what we were going to buy, word by word. It was really cute and lovely to see how seriously they took the task and wrote down in their own handwriting the ingredients for our meal.

Finally, we were all done and now it was time to get dressed. With the excitement in the air these little ones, my angels, were done in a second, dressed in no time. I do remember, I stood there and observed their little faces. Their excitement and commitment filled me with pride and pure love. We were all ready, took the shopping bags and of course the money and the car keys. To keep the excitement going, meaning to stay on the same level, I put our music on (their music really) 'the wheels on the bus go round...' they sang the whole way to the supermarket, happy and excited.

Arriving at the place we took out our shopping list and followed the list step by step. Of course, it took us a while to do the shopping but for them it was an important task and they felt very much in charge and in control of the process. At the end they asked if they could have something for themselves, a little treat. I said yes, let's finish the shopping list and see what we can find for all of us. I led them to what I thought would be good for them, by showing them the treats that I had chosen already in my mind. Of course they tried other treats and of course I led them to my 'treats'. They always had two choices to choose from.

Satisfied and fulfilled with our mission we were in the car ready to drive home. Different music on the way home: I always played classical music like Mozart to surround them with calmness and relaxation. Going shopping and being on it for a long period of time can be quite exhausting for them and me.

Our shopping experience was like this every time we went shopping and it became a lovely ritual. What I am saying here is, when you use your creativity in a way that comes naturally, everything around you becomes easy. The new experience shapes and forms a tool that becomes more clear and real to you. With time you can reuse it over and over again, share and pass it on to others.

I mention in this book a lot of great tools that you can use and start to collect for your own magic box. Each chapter has its own tool to be taken, shaped and formed with your unique sparkles.

You are your own magic – spread out these sparkles and make the world glitter in all colours!

I AM LIFE

CHAPTER FOURTEEN

Enjoy And Have Fun On The Way

IS LIFE too serious or are you making your life quite serious? Life can become serious when we are rushing around like headless chickens, using the words 'I am busy': busy with work, busy with kids, busy cleaning up, busy cooking, busy paying the bills, busy with catching up on stuff etc. Actually life should have a smile on its face and whatever we do, we ought to have some kind of fun and enjoyment in what we do or even love what we do. Please just stop for a moment. Wherever you are. Breathe and recognise what is around you:

- ❧ **The fresh air that is filling your lungs**
- ❧ **The sun that is bringing warmth and life to you, to all of us**
- ❧ **The sky with its uninterrupted view with no end**
- ❧ **The flowers with their unique shapes, colours and smells**

ভ The butterflies with their amazing elegance

ভ The bees, going from one flower to the other

ভ The leaves with their peaceful sound in the wind

ভ The stars with their twinkles and sparkles

ভ The moon with its powerful light...

The list is endless. Reflect and focus on little things.

> *'Don't be pushed by your problems,*
> *be led by your dreams.'*
>
> *- Ralph Waldo Emmerson -*

Remember to make time for little things and to be in the present. It will put a smile on your face. A smile on the face will activate happy hormones. Happy hormones will push to connect with the 'young heart'. The 'young heart' feels like 'free spirit'... all kinds of great energy is around you... that can lead you to be spontaneous... **having fun** inside and outside.

> *'Sing like no one is listening,*
> *Love like you have never been hurt,*
> *Dance like nobody is watching and*
> *Live like it is heaven on earth.'*
>
> *- Mark Twain -*

The feeling of fun is so vital today. Every part of your body is happy, excited and full of great energy. We all know that being 'busy' and 'getting stuff done' is part of life. However, if we can combine the busyness with fun and having a smile on our face, I think the colours around us would transform from dull to bright.

So, how to keep the fun part active and light? you might ask.

I would suggest using a routine or even perhaps a ritual for 'booking fun' – **me** time 100%. Everything and anything that you love will be booked for that day, it is your day. So you can't miss it. It can be:

☙ **daily if it is for a short period of time**

☙ **weekly if it is for a longer time**

☙ **monthly if you need a whole day, and so on**

You decide what is needed and design your **me** time. It is on your calendar pencilled in – a date with you and yourself. With this awareness you are creating a positive habit, a wonderful ritual, and nothing can take your smile away from your face.

Awareness + Positive Habit = Happy

Have fun by doing what you are doing. Enjoy your inner journey and also the outer journey. Being in a good place, feeling positive about yourself, will have the heart open all the time. Love and kindness, compassion and patience, is a good frequency to be surrounded by, remember the water experience in Chapter 2.

I shared with you some great insights, profound information about the paths on Mother Earth... your unseen journey with its cosmic energies, the universal laws. Having the knowledge and wisdom will open up another level of awareness, being able to dive into the subconscious and bring it to the surface. You are in charge of everything. Dream big, don't be afraid and don't let anyone stop you from moving forward. Learn from true leaders who have a big heart, kindness and compassion, ask for help when needed and follow your gut feelings. No one is perfect and nor are you.

Enjoy what you have here and now and look forward to what is coming towards you. It will be much bigger and more beautiful than you can ever imagine. In the meantime play, play with the energy that is given to you...

THANK YOU for being part of my life and I am feeling very grateful for being part of your life.

Please say to yourself and never ever forget...

I **AM** UNIQUE
I **AM** SPECIAL
I **AM** ME

View at *www.jasminkahansson.com*

A Little Note For You

You perhaps asked yourself what I mean by astrology...

When you were born, the stars were aligned in a certain way. The universal energy at that precise moment in time is set in your birth chart called 'Map of Heaven'. With this energy, a certain temperament/colour is in you, that is mirrored from above... your beautiful self, ready to explore, challenge and grow on Mother Earth to achieve exactly what you need for yourself on your path – your authentic self, is all in your 'Map of Heaven'.

The inner play between consciousness and unconsciousness in yourself is a dance at different levels that shows the changes in your life, the challenges that you can, with awareness, turn into opportunities. The tension or pain that you experience on your path pushes you to reconnect with that source. To find the strength to overcome and transform yourself that will move you forward to your purpose, the goal – your authentic self.

About The Author

Jasminka Hansson has studied astrology all her life. She is a specialist in revealing a person's inner abilities and authentic ways and has helped women all over the world to regain their power and momentum in life. She does this by increasing their awareness about themselves and their lives to enable a more balanced and harmonious life. Through her teachings she also works with parents and their little ones to enhance their understanding of the family dynamics and how to best nurture the loved ones for a more successful representation of their uniqueness.

As a citizen of Europe and now residing in the UK, Jasminka is a seasoned artist who expresses her inner world through colours on canvas. She is a devoted mother and wife, and runs a successful health centre with her husband. She consults with private clients and is planning to run weekend retreats later this year.

She is a student of astrology, personal development and of the universal forces acting upon us.

Jasminka lives with her family in Dorset and travels regularly to Vienna and beyond. Jasminka's paintings can be viewed in colour at *www.jasminkahansson.com*